Startup Masterclass

Spark disruptive change and lead the future with your startup

Saurabh Jain

bpb

www.bpbonline.com

FIRST EDITION 2024

ISBN: 978-93-55516-473

Distributors:

BPB PUBLICATIONS
20, Ansari Road, Darya Ganj
New Delhi-110002
Ph: 23254990 / 23254991

DECCAN AGENCIES
4-3-329, Bank Street,
Hyderabad-500195
Ph: 24756967 / 24756400

MICRO MEDIA
Shop No. 5, Mahendra Chambers,
150 DN Rd. Next to Capital Cinema,
V.T. (C.S.T.) Station, MUMBAI-400 001
Ph: 22078296 / 22078297

To View Complete BPB Publications Catalogue Scan the QR Code:

Published by Manish Jain for BPB Publications, 20 Ansari Road, Darya Ganj, New Delhi-110002 and Printed by him at Manipal Technologies, Manipal

www.bpbonline.com

Dedicated to

My father and brother for inspiring me to be an entrepreneur.
To my mother and wife for supporting me always.
Special thanks to my guru, ***Vijay Shekhar Sharma****, without whom this book could not have been written.*

Forewords

The startup ecosystem in our country has grown leaps and bounds over the last few years, with young and bold changemakers driving the narrative of a new India. Today, India is at the forefront of technological advancements, and starting up is not a distant reality anymore. As we go forward, it is pertinent that the young get to learn everything about building a business, the glory of it all while also understanding how to deal with the problems that come your way. Here's where Saurabh's book *Startup Masterclass* comes into the picture. Having known him for years, which includes the time he spent working with Paytm, I have seen him working closely with many young entrepreneurs and guiding them along the way.

Startup Masterclass is a compelling book that will be a ready reckoner for those who are dreaming of starting up and are leading the wave of innovation in our country. Right from the definition of a start-up, to defining a product market fix, straight down to calculating market share, the book covers all aspects that need consideration. Here's hoping that this book helps many young entrepreneurs across the country, solve one problem at a time.

- Vijay Shekhar Sharma
*Founder and CEO, **Paytm***

It's been over 5 years since I have known Saurabh, we worked and did a few projects together. Beyond work, I have witnessed Saurabh's ability to mentor, coach, and collaborate with entrepreneurs, investors, and even policymakers. He adeptly translates global concepts into an Indian context, presenting them in visually backed, easy-to-understand snippets. This was one of the reasons he led the **Paytm - Build for India** initiative.

Startup Masterclass spans across the creators' journey answering questions he may have, and offers stages, a structure, vocabulary, theories, and examples in this book. Saurabh has brought in his understanding of the pulse of the Indian market, consumers, and digital trends to share with his readers. He has written about how these trends are getting localised for the Indian context, and where founders need to pay attention to these shifts, and where they can simply follow the global rule books. Finally, the book also unveils a few concepts and areas like types of intelligence, Equities/ESOPs, Taxation, and more, which Indian founders typically miss while planning their startup journeys. Earlier, Saurabh encouraged many early founders through offline sessions, and now the book would do the same or better. Enabling him to reach and help the founders take the plunge, speed up their pace, or build larger businesses.

- Bhushan Patil
*Founder, **Multiply Ventures** (VC Firm)*
*Ex-President, **Paytm***
*Ex-Director, **Alibaba.com***

About the Author

Saurabh Jain is a renowned mentor across startup incubators in India. He is an international speaker who has spoken at various international conferences including the SXSW and SXSW Edu in USA and in various IITs, IIMs and institutions of repute in India.

Saurabh Jain was Vice President in Paytm from 2018 to 2021 and has been an entrepreneur ever since. He is a senior member of various committees and organizations working in promotion of entrepreneurship and startup incubation across India.

Acknowledgement

I want to express my deepest gratitude to my family members for their unwavering support and encouragement throughout this book's writing, especially my mother and my wife.

I would also like to thank my team at Fun2Do Labs which helped me in the process of designing images for this book.

I am also grateful to BPB Publications for their guidance and expertise in bringing this book to fruition. It was a long journey of revising this book, with valuable participation and collaboration of reviewers, technical experts, and editors.

I would also like to acknowledge the valuable contributions of my colleagues and co-workers during many years working in Paytm, who have taught me so much and provided valuable feedback on my work. Special thanks to Deepak Abbot, Bhushan Patil, Amit Singhal and other senior folks in the industry who helped me verify the facts written in the book.

Finally, I would like to thank all the readers who have taken an interest in my book and for their support in making it a reality. Your encouragement has been invaluable.

Preface

Over the last 6 years, I have attended lots of startup events as a speaker and have met hundreds of startup entrepreneurs. I have observed that most startup entrepreneurs do not know the formula for creating a successful startup. Before joining Paytm as Vice President in 2018, as a startup entrepreneur myself, I began searching for the formula to build a successful startup. In 2015 when I visited San Francisco and in parallel read the book – 'The Lean Startup', I realised that there is a formula behind successful startups. Prior to that even after running multiple startups for years I was sort of lost in this endless maze of buzzwords and media hype around startups.

Since 2015, I have read more than 200 books to research the best procedure for creating a winning startup. As luck would have it, one of India's most successful startup entrepreneurs, Mr Vijay Shekhar Sharma, founder of Paytm (India's highest-valued unicorn startup in 2020 and a big, listed company now) also gave me the opportunity to work directly under him and learn from him. I also learned a lot from people in the startup ecosystem with whom I had the good fortune to meet while being a speaker at a large number of startup events in India.

I realised the need to share my knowledge with entrepreneurs around the world. If people who learn startup best practices do not share them then the new entrepreneurs will not be able to learn them fast. They will have to go through the long process of trial and error. Covid has shown that we have to increase the pace of innovation. We need to solve the problems of Earth before becoming an interplanetary species one day.

Thus, I am sharing this knowledge because my grandfather used to say that knowledge increases when you share it. I am giving you whatever I learned related to startups. I do not want anything back. Just share this knowledge wherever you can. Let us build for the world together.

In this book we will be looking at the following aspects of starting a startup through each chapter:

Chapter 1: Introduction to Startup Canvas- This chapter will give you an introduction to the visual tool I have created for understanding startup lifecycle. This tool is called 'Startup Canvas'.

Chapter 2: Product- Developing a successful product is one of the most important goals of a startup. This chapter will give you an introduction to the important concepts of product management.

Chapter 3: People- Great products can only be developed by recruiting great talent in the startup. In this chapter we learn about the issues to keep in mind while recruiting co-founders and core team members. We also discuss things to keep in mind while scaling up the organisation.

Chapter 4: Purchasing Power- Any startup requires a lot of money and resources to function. Thus, a startup needs to focus on increasing its purchasing power. In this chapter we will learn about the bootstrapping phase and getting funding from angel investors and venture capitalists. We also learn about the steps in creating a great pitch deck and points to keep in mind while signing a term sheet.

Chapter 5: Conclusion: When Should I Start a Startup - Starting a startup is one of the most difficult decisions of any entrepreneur's life. In this chapter I try to explore the best time to start a startup.

As an entrepreneur, I have learned a lot over the years. Even in my role as Vice President of Paytm I learned a lot from Vijay Shekhar Sharma and his team. This book is a way of sharing those learnings with you the reader. I hope you learn from this book and go on to create a world changing startup.

Coloured Images

Please follow the link to download the
Coloured Images of the book:

https://rebrand.ly/8ms7q5u

We have code bundles from our rich catalogue of books and videos available at **https://github.com/bpbpublications**. Check them out!

Errata

We take immense pride in our work at BPB Publications and follow best practices to ensure the accuracy of our content to provide with an indulging reading experience to our subscribers. Our readers are our mirrors, and we use their inputs to reflect and improve upon human errors, if any, that may have occurred during the publishing processes involved. To let us maintain the quality and help us reach out to any readers who might be having difficulties due to any unforeseen errors, please write to us at :

errata@bpbonline.com

Your support, suggestions and feedbacks are highly appreciated by the BPB Publications' Family.

Piracy

If you come across any illegal copies of our works in any form on the internet, we would be grateful if you would provide us with the location address or website name. Please contact us at **business@bpbonline.com** with a link to the material.

If you are interested in becoming an author

If there is a topic that you have expertise in, and you are interested in either writing or contributing to a book, please visit **www.bpbonline.com**. We have worked with thousands of developers and tech professionals, just like you, to help them share their insights with the global tech community. You can make a general application, apply for a specific hot topic that we are recruiting an author for, or submit your own idea.

Reviews

Please leave a review. Once you have read and used this book, why not leave a review on the site that you purchased it from? Potential readers can then see and use your unbiased opinion to make purchase decisions. We at BPB can understand what you think about our products, and our authors can see your feedback on their book. Thank you!

For more information about BPB, please visit **www.bpbonline.com**.

Table of Contents

CHAPTER 1

Introduction to Startup Canvas

Introduction

After distilling all the knowledge, I gathered over the last many years, I have created a visual tool to mentor budding startup founders. This tool is called **'Startup Canvas'**. Startup Canvas aims to help you plan your startup's journey in such a way, that you create a winning startup.

Startups are incredibly complex, and they operate through an even more complex environment, yet we can see that the actions and decisions of winning entrepreneurs are never by chance or accidental. They too, follow the best practices that they have learned. Learning and following those practices is not possible for a new entrepreneur in a short time but my aim is to provide a comfortable starting point to a new entrepreneur so that he or she can start on the right path and learn the appropriate things, with time.

Most startup entrepreneurs are like *Abhimanyu* (from the legendary Indian epic *Mahabharata*). He knew how to go into battle but did not know the correct way of coming out of it. I, in a way relate to *Abhimanyu*, here. Reading 200+ books and working with *Mr. Vijay Shekhar Sharma* in Paytm while also meeting lots of successful startup investors and founders, gave me access to the winning formula for growing a startup.

Figure 1.1: Startup canvas

This book is called *Startup Masterclass* and it aims to mentor you, a budding entrepreneur in your quest for building a successful startup.

To make you understand the startup lifecycle in detail, I have created a tool called **Startup Canvas**. It is intended to create an understanding of the appropriate best practices at every stage of startup lifecycle.

Structure

This chapter covers the following topics:

- Who is an entrepreneur?
- What is a startup?
- Value mountain
- 3 goals of a startup
- 3 focus areas of startup founders
- 3 stages of startup life cycle
- Startup canvas
- Types of startups

Objectives

This chapter will introduce you to terms like entrepreneur, startup and value mountain. The chapter will also introduce you to the startup lifecycle and **Startup Canvas**, a tool to understand the startup lifecycle. The chapter will end with the introduction to various types of startups.

Who is an entrepreneur?

Entrepreneur is a buzzword these days. The media extensively covers successful entrepreneurs like *Elon Musk* and *Jeff Bezos* and portrays them as new-age gods. Many youngsters do not want to be job seekers these days. They want to be entrepreneurs. Unfortunately, not many understand the meaning of the word entrepreneur. Many do not understand the difference between being an entrepreneur and a person running a business.

Figure 1.2: *Entrepreneur*

We relate the word entrepreneur with high-tech startups and the modern era. You would be surprised to learn that economists have been studying this word for 300 years. *Entrepreneur* is in fact an old French word which English borrowed.

Till some time ago, I understood an entrepreneur as an individual who has an active role in founding a startup along with a tangible ownership in that startup. *John Doerr* is one of the most legendary investors in Silicon Valley and is also one of the earliest investors in both Google and Amazon. According to him:

> *Entrepreneur is someone who does more than anyone thinks possible with less than anyone thinks possible.*

This definition is one of the best definitions of the word Entrepreneur. It made it clear that entrepreneurs can be anywhere. While we all relate entrepreneurship with startups this definition makes it clear that entrepreneurs can be outside of startups too. They do not need to be running startups. A good example is *Mukesh Ambani* (the richest man in India in 2020). He is the most iconic entrepreneur in India, yet he is running an old company that has been in existence for many decades.

I personally believe that **Artificial Intelligence (AI)** and other technologies will take over most of the existing jobs in the coming decades. The only viable career option in the coming decades will be entrepreneurship or intrapreneurship (working in the founding team or senior position in a startup). Technology and changing digital lifestyles will disrupt all existing businesses. Only entrepreneurs will thrive in this disruption. Thus, the future belongs to the entrepreneurs.

What is a startup?

In the last 10 years **startup** is one of the fastest growing words in popularity. Most people did not know about the word **startup** a decade ago. Startups like Uber, Stripe and Paytm, etc., have made this word famous. Government programs like **Startup India** have also increased their popularity. Despite its huge popularity, no one seems to know the exact meaning of the word **startup**.

Figure 1.3: *What is a Startup?*

Interestingly, people who work in big startups also do not know whether they work in a corporation or a startup. When I joined Paytm (which was India's highest-valued startup in 2020) as Vice President in 2018, I met a lady who was one of the earliest employees in the company. She asked me if Paytm was still a startup even though it had thousands of employees. For her startups meant small fast-growing companies.

Most people do not have clarity on what a startup is. Some people believe that every small company is a startup. While some believe that every new organization is a startup, others believe that all medium and small businesses can be classified as startups. You may be surprised to know that some believe freelancers to be startups, as well. Some believe that startups are only about technology. Thus, there is a lot of confusion on the meaning of the term startup among people.

Steve Blank, the author of **The Startup Owner's Manual** and a global startup mentor has provided the following definition of a startup:

> *A startup is a temporary organisation in search of a scalable, repeatable, profitable business model.*

He says in his book that startups are not the smaller versions of large companies. Startups are different from big corporations. They want to find a scalable, repeatable, and profitable business model. According to *Blank*, they are temporary organizations. Either they grow big and become corporations or they die. Thus, startups cannot always remain a startup.

Steve's definition is good, but it does not cover some bigger startups who already have found a scalable, repeatable and profitable business model but still are called startups by people in industry and media.

Also, Steve's definition does not cover new ventures by existing corporations even though they may be acting like startups. For example, Reliance Jio in India disrupted the telecom industry in India even though it was the last entrant in the industry. Reliance is one of the biggest private sector companies in India (in 2023) but its telecom venture Jio acted like a startup and dislodged the incumbents.

I personally like the definition provided by *Eric Ries*, the author of **The Lean Startup**:

> *A startup is a human institution designed to deliver a new product or service under conditions of extreme uncertainty.*

Eric's definition is agnostic to the size of a startup. It is also agnostic to the lifecycle stage of a startup. He simply focuses on delivering a new product or a service under the conditions of extreme uncertainty. If we take *Eric's* definition, we will be able to justify Uber, Paytm and Reliance Jio to be startups even though they are not small and temporary organisations.

Over the last 4 years, I have met hundreds of startup founders and have formed my own definition of a startup. According to me, a startup can be defined as:

> *One or more individuals trying to solve problem(s) by creating product(s) or service(s) in a scalable way.*

My definition focuses on problem solving. I found that successful startups focus on solving the problems of users. Also, successful startups find a scalable solution to these problems. A startup can be a company, an organization or even an open-source project. Thus, I have defined a startup to be a group of individuals. The individuals may be working in a formal or informal setting. We have seen how Wikipedia and WordPress have changed the world despite their open-source roots.

Startups are the disruptors. In the 21st century, change and uncertainty are on the rise. Humans are facing newer problems, whether it is space exploration or the development of solutions to COVID, startups have now become critical to the growth and well-being of our society. Whatever the problem, a startup nearly always has a scalable solution to it. Thus, startups are here to stay.

Value mountain

An entrepreneur's direction is guided by the **value mountain**. Mountain is a metaphor for the challenging work which a startup must do in order to get a large amount of value.

***Figure 1.4:** Value mountain*

Running a startup is one of the toughest challenges you will face in your life. It will be like climbing a mountain. However, you should not choose *any* mountain to climb. It should be a mountain which excites you and that which provides you with treasure when you reach the top.

Thus, before beginning your startup journey, assess calmly if you can embark on this perilous journey or not. Moreover, discuss the difficult journey to come with your family and close friends. Your family's support is immensely important in this difficult journey. Thus, they should fully support you in this journey.

Moreover, try to analyze the **value** you will be creating at the end of this difficult journey. If the value created is not big enough, do not embark on this journey. Do not venture on a startup journey, just to be self-employed. Running a startup is way more difficult than one can anticipate.

Thus, start a startup only if you can climb the value mountain and take the treasure on top of it.

3 goals of a startup

A startup founder has lots of dreams. Those dreams would only come true if the startup founder executes his plan properly. To be able to execute properly, the founder needs to have explicit goals. These goals need to be kept to a minimum as it is humanly impossible to achieve a large number of goals.

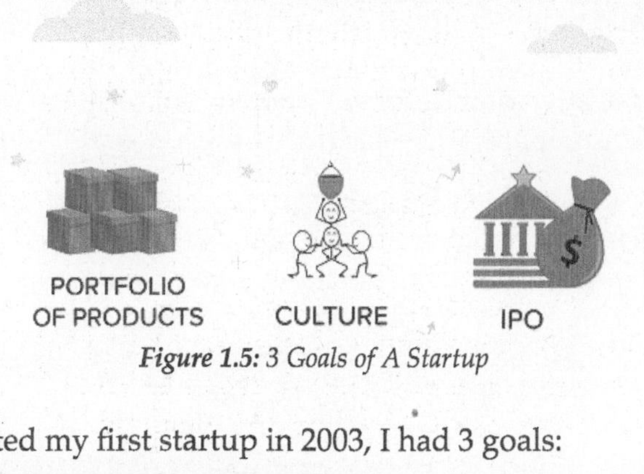

Figure 1.5: *3 Goals of A Startup*

When I started my first startup in 2003, I had 3 goals:

- Portfolio of successful products
- Iconic organizational culture
- IPO

I wanted to create a **portfolio of successful products**. I admired Microsoft and Google a lot at that time and had the dream that one day my startup would be able to achieve this goal. **What I did not know was, that to achieve this goal I would need to focus on solving one or more problems of the users.** I wanted to create a portfolio of successful products but without any good problem(s) to solve, I did not find any good solution(s). I learned this lesson in the long run, after great difficulty and multiple setbacks.

The second thing I wanted was an **iconic organizational culture**. I wanted people in my startup to feel happy and motivated to do something big. I had heard about iconic cultures in companies based in Silicon Valley companies and wanted my startup to also have that kind of culture. Only after working for more than 10 years, I learned that culture is something you need to nurture carefully, so that it lasts the long run. Cultures cannot be bought or copied; you need to invest time and plenty of effort into building it, from day one.

The third big dream of any startup founder is **Initial Public Offering (IPO)**. I also dreamt of having a successful IPO one day and becoming a millionaire or billionaire. Moreover, IPO may be the most glamorous thing to happen to a startup, but it is achieved by only a very few selected startups who are able to scale big. For scaling big, you need to achieve the first two goals.

There can be other goals, but I strongly feel that any commercial startup needs to have these three goals. Many entrepreneurs create a startup with the explicit goal of selling it to a bigger company like Google. While that may make you wealthy, on the other hand if you truly want to be successful, you need to achieve these 3 goals. Take the case of Apple, Microsoft, Google, Amazon, etc., and you will find that all successful companies have achieved these 3 goals.

In my new startup, I am focusing on these three goals from day one and would like to attain them as soon as possible. In my very first startup, I had dreams to achieve these goals but no plan or execution to achieve them. In my current startup, I have a single-minded focus on achieving these as soon as possible. Attaining these should be the number one priority of any startup founder.

3 focus areas of startup founders

As a budding entrepreneur, you have lots of choices when it comes to spending your time, along with your precious and limited resources.

I have learned that the 3 of the most important areas to focus on, for a budding entrepreneur are (refer to *Figure 1.6*):

- Product
- People
- Purchasing power

***Figure 1.6**: 3 Focus areas of startup founders*

These 3 Ps are the 3 main steps on our road towards our three goals. I have also seen that winning entrepreneurs like the founder of Paytm, are good at these three tasks.

Product

Every startup needs to create one or more products that solve some problems for the users and the customers. Without creating a good product with paying consumers, no startup can grow and become profitable.

People

To create the winning product(s) you need to assemble a team that can execute well. Thus, any successful startup requires good employees and successful startup founders, as good recruiters and motivators.

Purchasing power

Every startup needs money to purchase the time of its people and the essential resources required to create and provide products to customers. Some startups do not buy products using money from investors or founders, but they purchase them using other mechanisms like ESOPs, crowdfunding, and barter. Thus, the term, purchasing power instead of money or fund raising.

As a founder, focus your time honing these three skills required for your startup to succeed. Time and focus are bigger constraints than money which I had seen in action as the Vice President of Paytm. You can get the money from outside, but you always have limited time and focus, thus, a startup founder should be focused on these three areas that we discussed above.

3 stages of startup life cycle

Most people associate startups with scaling. The media has a habit of covering startups that have secured funding and are scaling fast. Due to this habit of the media, most people feel that startups are only about scaling. Scaling is the stage in which the external world at large comes to know about the company. A large part of the startup lifecycle is not visible to the external world. In total there are three stages of the startup lifecycle (refer to *Figure 1.7*):

- Search
- Build
- Scale

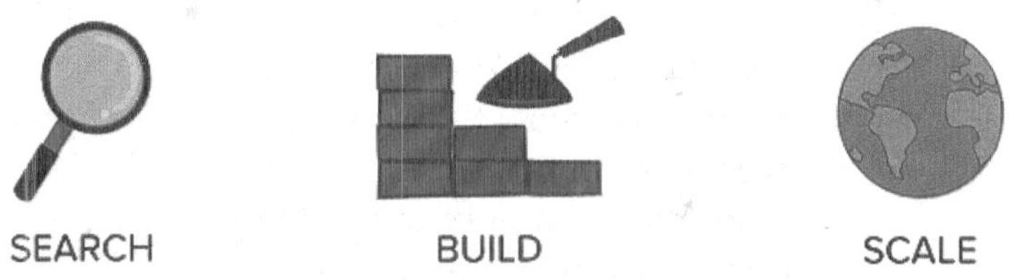

Figure 1.7: *3 Stages of startup life cycle*

Search

The first phase of the startup lifecycle is **search**. A startup needs to first, find a problem and then a solution to that problem. A major reason for the failure of startups is building products that people do not want. Searching for a big problem and creating a solution around that problem helps in providing a strong foundation to the startup for future success. This stage ends when the startup has found **Problem Solution Fit.**

This stage generally requires just the co-founders to work on finding the problem and creating a prototype solution to solve this issue. The aim is to find a **scaling pattern** which can solve this. In some cases, 1-2 employees can be recruited but at this stage, entrepreneurs need to bootstrap (spend their own money), and big expenses need to be curtailed.

To explain this, let us take an example of a food startup. If we were creating a food startup, we would first need to find a big, food related problem that customers face. Say the problem selected is getting healthy fast food.

The second step will be to search for solutions to this problem globally. The founders should experiment with a few solutions of their own.

A part of finding a good solution will be to find a scaling pattern. **Scaling pattern** is the pattern language for the potential solution. Having a scaling pattern is important to understand the scalability potential of a product.

An example of a solution for a startup focusing on healthy fast food can be **Healthy Burger** (wheat or multigrain bun with fresh vegetables as a filling). Another solution can be the South Indian dish **Idli-Sambar**. Both the solutions are very different. Startups can focus on any one of them and create a suite of products around this solution.

For example, if a startup wants to create a healthy burger, then it can create a menu with different kinds of healthy burgers. It can create burgers with local vegetables to suit local tastes and thus, expand globally. It can also have multiple varieties of buns. Moreover, constraining the solution to just healthy burgers gives the startup the required efficiency in execution and focus. Thinking of the healthy burger as a pattern allows the startup to create a suite of healthy burgers to suit all kinds of locales and tastes.

Similarly, if the startup chooses ***Idli-Sambar*** as the dish, it can experiment with different kinds of doughs for creating *Idli* to suit different locales. Also, it can experiment with different kinds of *chutneys* (Indian sauces) to compliment the *Idlis* to suit all tastes.

A blunder any startup can make is to think that it can give 5 different types of products to consumers as a solution. If the startup provides healthy burgers and *idli sambar* in the same shop the logistics of providing both will make it difficult to achieve economies of scale while also creating challenges in the making of **Standard Operating**

Procedures (SOPs). Providing five types of burgers or *idlis* is easier than providing 5 different dishes simultaneously.

Thus, focusing on one solution and its multiple variations can provide efficiency in execution and fulfilling consumer choices as well. When the startup founder(s) find a good scaling pattern, we can say that that startup has achieved a **problem solution fit**.

During this stage, the startup's founders are generally finalized. It is generally rare to get funding during this stage and thus the founders must bootstrap (fund the startup with their own money) the startup at this stage. Nowadays, a startup can try to get some grants from incubators and the government under various startup funding schemes.

Build

Once a startup finds a problem and builds a solution for the problem and achieves the problem solution fit it needs to recruit a small core team that can iteratively build a product. This stage goes on till the startup achieves **Product Market Fit.**

At the beginning of this stage, some angel investors can be approached for a little bit of funding as the startup has something to showcase to them since it has already achieved the **problem solution fit.**

Every startup must create a **Minimum Viable Product (MVP)** and start selling it in the market. Startups need to focus on 2 things in this stage: **making** and **selling.** The startup must iteratively increase features of MVP through feedback it receives from actual users and customers. Additionally, the startup also must learn about the various details of the market like market size, market structure, the barrier to entry, etc.

Product market fit is a stage where the product is so good that consumers want to use the product themselves without a lot of push. For example, when using Uber for the first time, I had the urge to use it repeatedly. That was Uber's product reaching the product market fit. However, this usually takes time and may involve multiple iterations to the product.

Scale

Once the product is desired by the market, it becomes easy to get money from venture capitalists and big angels. It is a good time to scale the startup. At this stage, a startup must transform into a corporation. Many people may need to be recruited and a formal structure needs to be put into place. Uber, Paytm, etc., have taken this route once they achieved the product market fit.

Thus, we see that all 3 stages of startups are very critical. **Startup founder(s) should not try to scale from day 1 before achieving the problem solution fit and product market fit.** Therefore, any startup whether big or small must follow the 3 stages of the startup lifecycle and start with the **search** stage, follow up with the **build** stage and then finally **scale** the startup.

Startup canvas

Startup Canvas is a management tool which I have created for informing startup founders of the journey of a startup. This tool was built using extensive research and was validated by various entrepreneurs, angel investors and venture capitalists in my discussions with them.

Refer to *Figure 1.8* for an overview of this tool:

***Figure 1.8**: Startup canvas*

The tool focuses on three areas: **Product, People** and **Purchasing Power**. When combined with the 3 stages of startup lifecycle we get nine steps to startup success:

Product

The most important thing in a startup is the product that it creates. We can divide the product development into 3 phases:

- Problem Solution Fit
- Product Market Fit
- Growth Profit Fit

They have been elaborated in the following paragraphs:

Problem Solution Fit

As we already covered earlier, startups start with a figuring out a big problem and the founders try in the first phase to find the solution to that problem. When they successfully find such a solution and the way of scaling that solution conceptually, we say that they have found the **problem solution fit**.

Product Market Fit

Next, the startup starts to build the product. When the customers start pulling the product from the startup, we can say that the startup has achieved **'product market fit'**. At this stage the startup achieves high demand and retention for the product.

Growth Profit Fit

This is the final goal of a startup's product life cycle. A startup usually achieves this when a startup has scaled the product to have super growth over many years and it finally becomes profitable due to economies of scale.

People

A startup is made up of people. The founders are the most important people in a startup followed by the core team. After the startup grows it needs a large number of people to function as a corporation. We can divide **people management** into 3 distinct phases:

- Finding founders
- Finding core team
- Building corporation

Finding founders

Initially a startup founder should decide whether he or she needs a co-founder. In case co-founders are required, then usually co-founders should be finalized during the initial few months of a startup's life cycle. In some cases, co-founders can come later in the startup's life cycle according to the needs of product development or scaling.

Finding good co-founders is not easy and thus it should be done carefully and with adequate precaution.

Finding core team

Once a startup finalizes a broad conceptual solution and the problem to focus on then it should start to recruit a core team. The core team can range from 2 to 20 people depending on the complexity of the product and market but should not be very large.

The core team should be like STEM cells. When the human baby starts the journey of life the initial cells are generalist cells who have the ability to divide into specialized cells later on, if required. Your core team members should also be like that. They should be generalists in the initial phase and then become specialists when required later on in the startup's life cycle.

Building corporation

In the scaling phase a startup needs to ramp up quite fast and it will need a formal corporate structure at this stage. Without a formal corporate structure, it becomes difficult to manage a large number of people within an organization.

Purchasing power

Any startup needs purchasing power to function. the company needs money to not only pay salaries but to buy raw material and to create infrastructure where manpower can work efficiently. It can sometimes get resources without cash payments by paying in the form of shares or bartering with other organizations.

Management of purchasing power can also be divided into 3 phases, namely:

- Bootstrapping

- Getting Angel Investment
- Getting Venture Capital

Bootstrapping

A startup needs money to function. Initially only founders believe in the startup and thus a startup will not get money from outside investors. Hence, founders will need to invest their own money in the startup in the initial period. Sometimes they can get money from family and friends also during this phase as well.

Getting Angel Investment

Once a startup finds the problem solution fit it becomes easier for the startup to get money from professional investors called angel investors. There are the first set of professional investors who invest in the company. They generally invest based on the competence and goodwill of founders, scope of the problem and the scalability of the solution.

Getting Venture Capital

Finally, once a startup achieves product market fit it becomes easy for a startup to get venture capital. Venture capitalists are a special kind of investors who provide risk capital at scale to startups in the form of venture capital.

These are the general phases in a startup's life cycle. Any founder who wants to start a startup should have basic knowledge of these 9 phases of a startup's life cycle. All startup founders should have broad clarity of these phases and should plan their involvement, investment, and expectations accordingly.

Types of startups

Generally, when we think of startups, we instantly remember fast growing companies like Uber, Stripe or Paytm or their smaller fast-growing counterparts. Many people feel startups are only fast-growing, investor funded companies. While the most glamorous startups which are generally covered by the media do fall into this category.

Startups are in fact of multiple varieties. They can obviously be classified according to size, however the criteria should be that they be classified according to their goals for a better understanding of their differences.

Now, let us look at the four types of startups (refer to *Figure 1.9*):

- 'Winner takes all' startup
- Lifestyle startup
- Social startup
- Corporate startup

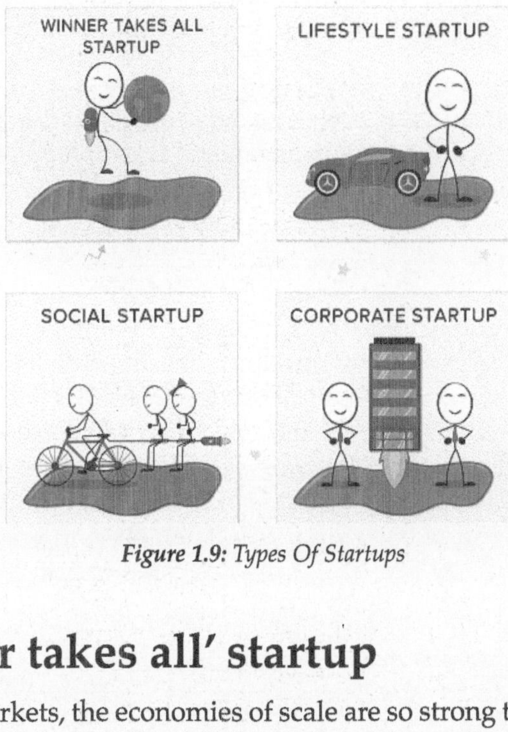

Figure 1.9: *Types Of Startups*

'Winner takes all' startup

In certain markets, the economies of scale are so strong that the winner usually takes the lion's share of the market. The market supports very few extremely large players. Thus, startups in those markets want to grow as much as they can to become the number 1 player. For this goal, they want as many resources as they can get. Startups like Uber fall into this category. I call these **'winner takes all'** startups.

Lifestyle startup

Some traditional businesses are very profitable, but they do not grow much. The founders are happy with these businesses and live a lavish lifestyle, but they do not grow like startups. These are called lifestyle businesses in startup jargon. These are businesses that cannot get startup investors as their growth potential is limited.

A new kind of startup has emerged which tries to provide a lavish lifestyle to the founders and people working in that startup. These startups also want to be extremely profitable and grow big in revenues and profit while still providing founders and employees with time to live a relaxed and luxurious lifestyle. **Basecamp** is a famous company that believes in this thought. I call these companies lifestyle startups.

Social startup

There are startups who want to change the world but do not want to make a profit. I call them social startups. These startups are a hybrid between 'not for profit' organizations and startups. Khan Academy is a good example of such a startup.

Corporate startup

Existing corporations sometimes create a new venture with the explicit aim to grow like a startup in a new line of business. Reliance Jio in India is a very good example of such a startup. Reliance is one of the largest companies in India which has disrupted the telecom industry through its telecom venture called Reliance Jio. Many people do not think of such corporate ventures as startups because these ventures start with large budgets and a big workforce. After reading the definition of startups provided by *Eric Ries* (author of **The Lean Startup**) :

> *A startup is a human institution designed to deliver a new product or service under conditions of extreme uncertainty.*

I feel that these ventures should also be called startups. These corporate ventures work under conditions of extreme uncertainty and aim to deliver a disruptive product or a service. Thus, they should ideally be termed as corporate startups.

Thus, we see that startups can be in various forms. When you are starting a startup, you should be clear about which type of startup you want to create and carry forward. Your initial choice about the type of startup you want to build will determine your course of action over the years.

Conclusion

Startups are changing the world. Entrepreneurship is becoming the career of choice. Creating a successful startup is not easy. We need proper direction to create a successful startup. We also need proper goals and a path towards execution of those goals. **Startup Canvas** acts as a tool to guide us in various stages of a startup lifecycle. Finally, we learned about the various types of startups.

Key terms

- **Entrepreneur:** Entrepreneur is someone who does more than anyone thinks possible with less than anyone thinks possible.
- **Startup:** One or more individuals trying to solve problem(s) by creating product(s) or service(s) in a scalable way.

Chapter 2
Product

Introduction

The most important thing a startup does for the external world is to create a great product. To create a great product, we need to first understand the meaning of the word product.

A product is any good, service, or information that can be offered to a market to satisfy a want or need.

Figure 2.1: Product

Thus, we see that a product can be a good, service, or even an intangible things like information. Gone are the days when products meant only physical products. Today, a product includes services or even information. In fact, with the advent of the internet, digital information-based products have grown rapidly.

Product is the most important focus area of the startup founder. Startup founders need to concentrate a lot on creating the best product in the market to solve a particular problem of the users and customers.

A good product gives a good **User Experience (UX).** A startup founder should try to understand the problems of the user (person who will use the product) and the customer (person who will pay for the product) and try to solve it in a way that the product gives the best possible user experience at a good price. Providing a good user experience is less about technology and more about understanding the psychology of the user.

Structure

We will be covering the following topics:

- Problem solution fit
- Which problem to focus on
- Ingredients of a great startup solution
- Scaling pattern
- Minimum Viable Product (MVP)
- Introduction to Agile Project Management
- Introduction to SCRUM
- Introduction to analytics
- Funnels
- Product management
- Market size
- Technology adoption life cycle
- Digital business models
- What is product market fit?
- When should your startup pivot?

- Growth profit fit
- Engines of growth for a startup
- Growth hacking
- Profit

Objectives

Product is the most important focus area for any startup. In this chapter we will learn the best practices related to product management. We will also learn about the 3 stages in product lifecycle: problem solution fit, product market fit and growth profit fit. We will also learn about minimum viable product and agile project management.

Problem solution fit

As per Startup Canvas the first step in product development is **Problem Solution Fit**. The first step towards creating a great product is to find a big problem for the potential users and customers (refer to *Figure 2.2*):

Figure 2.2: *Problem Solution Fit*

Your own problems can be a great starting point of finding big customer problems. Problems of people around you can also be a good starting point. United Nations 17 **Sustainable Development Goals (SDGs)** are also good starting points for finding global problems.

Once problems are found then the focus shifts to creating a great solution. A great startup solution needs to be desirable, viable and feasible.

A good startup solution also needs to be scalable. Once we find a scalable solution to a big problem of users and customers, we can say that we have found **problem solution fit**. It is a huge milestone as it gives provides clarity on things to come for a startup and it also helps angel investors to vet a startup for its investing potential.

Which problem should you focus on?

Over the years I have learned that successful startups begin with a big user and customer problem. The world is full of problems so finding problems to solve is generally not a big issue. The real problem for startup founder(s) is to find the right problem to focus on. Over the years, I tried to find the formula to choose the right problem to solve. While reading the book, **Ikigai: The Japanese Secret to a Long and Happy Life**, I saw a diagram which gave me the answer to this question.

This diagram asks four questions (refer to *Figure 2.3*):

- What do you love?
- What are you good at?
- What the world needs?
- What you can be paid for?

Figure 2.3*: Which problems to focus on?*

At the start of my career, I thought that focusing on technology would be good for my startup. That was not a wise decision as technology is ever changing and is never permanent. I learned with great difficulty that a startup founder should focus on a good problem to solve. A good problem is more long term and is like that life partner who remains with you for life.

The reason why we are not able to focus on any one thing for the long term is that the correct answer to one or more of these questions is not being provided by our focus area. If you love what you build, are the best at building it, the world needs it and is willing to pay for it, then there is no reason for you not to be able to create and sell the product. Building and selling are the two most important things in a startup. If you do them correctly, your startup will be successful.

What should you love?

Being successful, demands putting in a large amount of time. According to famous author, *Malcolm Gladwell's* 10,000-hour rule, you need to devote at least 10,000 hours to something to become world class. Thus, you need to love doing your work, otherwise, you will not be able to devote as much time to it. Moreover, you will find inner peace and happiness only if you love what you do. If a startup founder does not love his or her work, then the startup is doomed from day one. Thus, the problem should be in the domain that excites the entrepreneur.

What you are good at?

In this highly competitive world if you provide a solution in which you are not world-class then no one will buy your solution. Thus, you need to find a good problem whose solution you can build from the angles of design, commercial viability, and technical feasibility. If you do not know the problem domain, it will take you longer to create a world class solution.

What the world needs?

A big mistake which technical founders make is to focus on the latest buzzword technology. In the euphoria of using the latest technologies they at times forget that they will get the money only when someone purchases their product or at least uses it. **People do not buy or use technology. They buy products which solve their problems.** The product needs to do the job which the target user wants it to do. The product must contribute to alleviating the pain of the user and providing some utility.

The United Nations has published *17 Sustainable Development Goals (SDGs)* (refer to *Figure 2.4*). Some of the goals included are:

- No poverty
- Zero hunger
- Quality education
- Clean water and sanitation
- Affordable and clean energy

Figure 2.4: *UN's Sustainable Development Goals*

I believe that they serve as an appropriate initial step in identifying what the world truly requires.

What can you be paid for?

You also need to focus on the specific value proposition you are giving to the user. If your product is doing the right job, solving the real pain points, and providing useful gains then customers will be generally willing to pay. You also need to check for the state of the industry landscape and see the power of buyers to determine prices and the ability of users to find substitutes for your product. If the product provides a good value proposition and the buyer is not able to dictate terms, then you will be able to get paid for the product easily. This is the ultimate test, as without the ability to charge customers you will not be able to make revenue and profit.

Thus, we see that a good problem needs to have feasible answers to all the above 4 questions. If you find such a problem that motivates you as a founder, or something that you or your co-founders have experienced in the problem domain and this problem has a lot of potential demand for which the customer is willing to pay then you have found your sweet spot – your reason to live, the place where your needs, desires, ambitions, and satisfaction meet. You have found the right problem when you reach this comfortable position – your *Ikigai*.

Ingredients of a great startup solution

Many startup founders sprinkle a healthy dose of technology buzzwords to make their pitch seem better. I have talked to many investors to date, and most do not like buzzword stuffing in presentations. These days buzzwords like AI/ML, blockchain, crypto, cloud and IoT are used quite liberally by founders to make their startup seem on the cutting edge (refer to *Figure 2.5*):

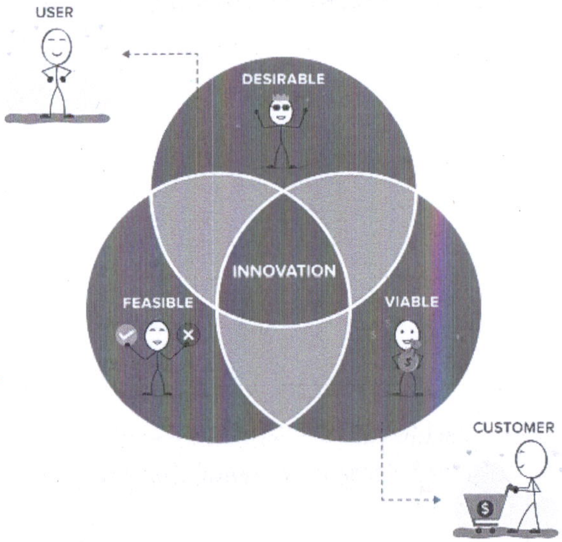

***Figure 2.5:** Ingredients of a great startup solution*

What many startup founders do not know and what most experienced investors know is that people pay for utility and not technology. Technology is worth only the utility it provides to the user or the customer. Thus, a startup founder should try to focus on the utility provided to the customer instead of focusing on the latest technology.

When we speak of the **user,** we are discussing the actual user of your product and the customer is the actual buyer of your product. For example, in case of an educational product the kid is the user, and the customer is the parent.

If a new technology provides more utility, then use that technology but do not stuff the latest technology in the solution to make it seem cutting edge even though the user may not feel delighted because of that. Any good product needs to be desirable, viable and feasible. Do not just focus on technology. Technology alone is just about technical feasibility. The more important goal is to make users feel good about using the product.

A good example of this is Zoom. Zoom became a hit in 2020 due to its simplicity and ease of use. Zoom has deep-pocketed rivals who are world-renowned for their technology, like Google, Microsoft and Facebook. Most people now prefer Zoom over them because of the good user experience. The reason is that users find Zoom and its features more desirable.

Any good product needs to be viable for the organization providing it. It should also be affordable for its customers. If the product is technically feasible but unaffordable by the customers, then it is consequential that the customers would not flock to buy it. Moreover, even if customers find the price point attractive but the solution ends up being expensive for the startup to provide, the startup will bleed money and eventually fold.

This should be differentiated from situations which demand economies of scale for achieving profitability. There are many markets and products which need a certain scale to become profitable. Thus, a startup will initially lose money in providing that solution but once it achieves the critical mass, it will start earning profits. Thus, when we are talking about viability, we are discussing long-term viability.

The supersonic plane *Concorde* was a good example of a product that was desirable and technically feasible but unviable from start. In the end, *Concorde* had to stop flying due to various reasons, lack of commercial viability being one of the primary reasons. Technology obviously plays a central role in any innovation, but the startup founder should remember that desirability and viability are equally important. The success of startups like Facebook, Zoom, Tesla, etc., has been there due to the focus of their founders to provide all 3 things – desirable product, viable product and feasible product, together in a unified whole.

Scaling pattern

The first step while developing a product is to find the right problem to solve for the user and the customer. The second step is to find a solution which is desirable, viable and feasible. Once the solution has been found the next step should be to explore the product's execution and scaling potential of the solution.

We should term this third step **scaling pattern** (refer to *Figure 2.6*):

Figure 2.6: *Scaling pattern*

Christopher Alexander introduced a concept called **pattern language** in the 1970s. It revolutionized the world of computing and design. After finding a good solution to the problem, the founder(s) should try to explore the pattern language of their potential solution. **Scaling pattern** is thus the pattern language that has been found for the potential solution.

A scaling pattern helps in finalizing the path a startup should take to solve the problem. Many times, like in the case of apps or food the same problem can be solved in multiple ways. **The founder(s) need to choose a clearly visible path to focus on.** To learn and experiment they can create internal prototypes to enhance their understanding. A big blunder many startups do is to focus on multiple paths with fewer available resources. A startup needs to concentrate on the chosen path after exploring all possible options.

The scaling pattern helps in expediting execution a lot. We used to be starved of design resources in my startup in 2015. Then we learned about pattern languages and started applying this concept. For a change, my small team was sitting idle 10% of the time because they improved their productivity, multiple times.

To understand the concept of pattern language, we will give you a few examples from the real world.

English can be used to write millions of blogs, but it contains only 26 alphabets. 26 alphabets can be combined in various ways into numerous words. These words can be combined to form sentences and these sentences can be combined to form paragraphs. These paragraphs then, combine to form blogs.

Thus, individual parts can form a bigger pattern which again can again be combined with such bigger patterns. These patterns can be formed at various levels. You will find ample examples in the real world and find such pattern languages everywhere. The pattern language of our body is that it is composed of cells, which form tissues, which form organs, which finally form the body.

Pattern languages provide a way of creating great variety with a few simple low-level structures. For example, DNA combines its building blocks in multiple ways to create a variety of life. The concept of a pattern language is used extensively in design, computer programming, governance, and more.

Take for example, a startup that wants to solve the problem of obesity due to consumer preference for fast food. Assume the startup has searched the problem domain and found 2 healthy fast-food options as potential solutions. The first option is *Healthy Burger* (wheat or multigrain bun with fresh vegetables as a filling). The second option is the South India dish, *Idli Sambar*.

Finding a scaling pattern will involve exploring the pattern language of *Healthy Burger* and *Idli Sambar*. Both solutions are very different. Our startup can focus on any one of them and create a suite of products around the solution.

If the startup wants to focus on the healthy burger, then it can create a menu with different kinds of healthy burgers. It can create burgers with local vegetables to suit local tastes and expand globally. It can also have multiple varieties of buns. Thus, constraining the solution to just healthy burgers gives the startup the required efficiency in execution and focus. Thinking of the healthy burger as a pattern allows the startup to create a suite of healthy burgers to suit all kinds of locales and tastes globally. The healthy burger can be customized at various levels. It can be customized at the level of the bun, the fillings, the spices or the packaging.

Similarly, if the startup chooses the *idli sambar* pattern it can experiment with different kinds of doughs for creating *idli* to suit different locales. We can also experiment with different kinds of *chutneys* (Indian sauces) to compliment *idlis* to suit all kinds of tastes.

A blunder any startup can do is to think that it can give 10 different types of products to consumers as a solution. If the startup provides healthy burgers and *idli sambar* in the same shop the logistics of providing both will make it difficult to achieve economies of scale and create challenges in the making of **Standard Operating Procedures**

(SOPs). Providing fives types of burgers or 5 types of *idlis* is easier than providing five different dishes simultaneously.

Thus, focusing on one solution and its multiple variations can bring efficiency in execution and simultaneously fulfil consumer choice. When startup founder(s) find a scaling pattern that has the following properties, we can say that the startup has achieved **problem solution fit**:

- **Scalable**
- **Practical**: Relatively easy to execute
- **Flexible**: Can create multiple desirable, viable and feasible solutions

This stage is very important in the lifecycle of a startup. At this stage, we can say that the startup has completed its search for a solution to the users/customers problem.

Minimum Viable Product (MVP)

A startup is always short of resources. In such a scenario, we must focus on creating the best possible product in the least amount of money. A big obstacle in creating a product that customers love is the lack of knowledge about the real needs of the customers. Thus, we need a way to reach out to real customers in the market as early as possible so that we can get knowledge about them. In the age of the internet, we cannot wait for months or years just for the first version of the product to come out in the market before we start getting feedback from the customers. In this situation, a concept called **Minimum Viable Product (MVP)** comes to our rescue (refer to *Figure 2.7*):

Figure 2.7: *Introduction to Minimum Viable Product*

Eric Ries in his book ***The Lean Startup*** introduced the concept of Minimum Viable Product. According to *Eric Ries*:

> *The minimum viable product is that version of a new product that allows a team to collect the maximum amount of validated learning about customers with the least effort.*

According to him, a startup is building a product under uncertainty. A startup needs to learn about and understand customer adoption as soon as possible to reduce uncertainty for the startup. The minimum viable product provides a mechanism for reaching out to customers early.

Ries also states that the minimum viable product can be updated through the Build | Measure | Learn feedback loop. Minimum Viable Product forms the starting point for taking the product to the market. The aim of the MVP is not to earn revenue but to learn as much as possible about the product's adoption risks. Thus, MVPs are more about earning knowledge than earning money (refer to *Figure 2.8*):

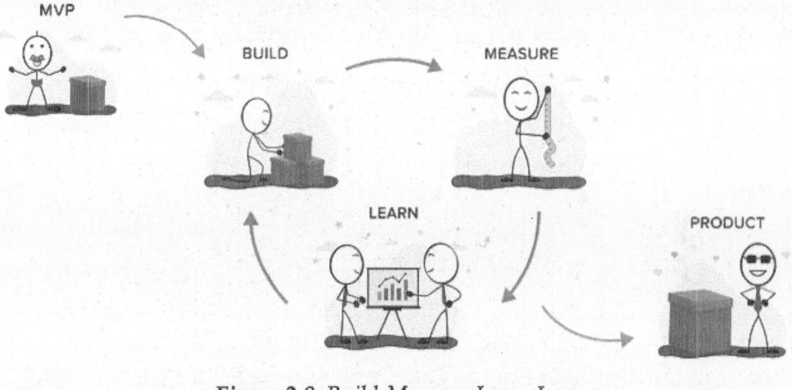

***Figure 2.8:** Build-Measure-Learn Loop*

I personally believe that we can also take inspiration from nature in understanding the minimum viable products. Babies are considered complete human beings even though they are missing many of the features expected in an average adult. Similarly, our products can be shared in the market in a complete way without many of the features required for a full-fledged product. We can add features based on customer feedback and usage data.

After multiple such build - measure - learn loops, a product attains maturity and people in the market usually start liking the product. Google has followed a similar process for Gmail over the years and

Uber has followed this process for its services. I practically saw first-hand that Paytm uses MVPs extensively.

The early evangelists who buy the MVP buy it because they feel something is better than nothing. They have a pressing problem and are usually happy even with a makeshift or an incomplete solution.

I would like to give you an example of an MVP in real life. Say if you want to start a startup like Uber. You do not need to start big and have an app on day one. In fact, the starting process can be quite simple and small.

You can just rent a registered taxi vehicle for 2-3 months and start with 1 cab which you yourself can drive. To get customers without any publicity or app you can just go to a small residential area like a group housing society or small colony. Most residential areas have a Resident Welfare Association (RWA) which has a WhatsApp group these days. You just need to get some way of sharing your number in such a group. People can just message you on WhatsApp or another popular messaging service in the local community and you can be available between specific times in that community on just a message or phone call.

This way you will interact with the customers directly and learn about the nuances of running an on-demand cab business yourself. Unlike customer interaction techniques used by big corporations, focused research groups or questionnaires, you are getting feedback from customers directly in real-world situations.

You can hire more drivers and cabs as the demand grows. You can create an app once you start getting many customers and you need to expand geographically. Thus, MVP helps in learning about customer and real-world problems at a fast pace with low expenses. Companies like Google and Paytm also use minimum viable products a lot. I have personally seen the concept being used at Paytm multiple times. Thus, I would recommend all startups to start with a minimum viable product and build the product iteratively.

Introduction to Agile Project Management

When I started my startup, I had a tough time completing projects on time. Somehow, we were always late. After many years I bumped into a process called **Agile**. Agile is a way of managing work. It is an easy process to understand and a relatively light weight process in execution. Agile Manifesto (**agilemanifesto.org**) is the guiding spirit of agile project management (refer to *Figure 2.9*):

***Figure 2.9**: Introduction to Agile Project Management*

Agile is a term that includes lots of project management techniques. SCRUM is the most famous among them. Extreme programming is another. Many people get into Agile thinking it is a watertight methodology.

I have used Agile for many years now and read many books on it and have attended many meetups and workshops. My own take is that Agile can be summed up in Indian Saint *Kabeer's* couplet:

काल करे सो आज कर, आज करे सो अब,

पल में प्रलय होएगा, बहुरि करेगा कब!!

Instead of tomorrow, do the work today; instead of today, do the work right now; death will come any moment, listener, how will you finish the work?

Agile is not a process but a way of thinking. It is about prioritizing and doing the most important work today instead of spending a long-time planning or procrastinating. Agile also tries to reduce time wastage in unnecessary planning, documentation, and meetings. Agile also tells that the customer is always right, and that products should be built as per his or her needs.

Agile has been very successful in startups across the world over the last 2 decades. Companies like Google and Paytm use it extensively. My favorite book on this topic is ***Scrum: A revolutionary approach to building teams, beating deadlines, and boosting productivity*** by *Jeff Sutherland.*

Introduction to SCRUM

SCRUM is one of the most popular techniques in agile project management. I would recommend the book **SCRUM - A revolutionary approach to building teams, beating deadlines and boosting productivity** to you. Here I am sharing a small summary of SCRUM from this book (refer to *Figure 2.10*):

***Figure 2.10**: Introduction to SCRUM*

Key concepts

Some key concepts related to SCRUM are:

1. **Product owner**: Product owner is the person who has the vision of what the team is going to accomplish or create.
2. **Team**: SCRUM works in teams. Team consists of people who will make the product owner's vision into reality. The team should consist of people with all the required skills to make the vision into reality.
3. **SCRUM master**: SCRUM Master is the person who coaches the team on Scrum framework. He helps the team eliminate anything that slows them down.
4. **Product backlog**: This is the list which tells at a high level what needs to be built or done to achieve the vision. The tasks in the product backlog need to be prioritized by the product owner after consultation with the team. The product backlog acts as a product road map for the team.

   The tasks in the product backlog need to be estimated for the effort each task will take. The effort needs to be estimated by relative size. For example, small, medium, and large etc. The effort required in completing each task should not be estimated in terms of the number of hours people will take to complete the task as that is very difficult to estimate exactly. Also, no two people will complete the same task in the same time.

   A more professional way of defining the effort required for each work item or task is to give points to each task based on the effort required. The points can be given in lengths defined by the Fibonacci sequence: 1, 2, 3, 5, 8 etc.
5. **Sprint**: The work in SCRUM is done in fixed periods of time. Each such fixed period is called a **Sprint**. Work is divided into multiple sprints of usually 1 or 2 weeks. Maximum length of a sprint is usually 1 month.

   At the start of a sprint the team targets the number of points it will finish in the sprint. This is the **Sprint Goal**.

   The team measures the tasks it was able to complete in a sprint by adding points of the tasks it completed in a sprint. The total points achieved in a sprint is called **velocity**. The team aims to increase the velocity in each subsequent sprint.

   The team should be completely autonomous during a sprint and no task can be added or deleted once the sprint is started.

Sprint also needs planning. Before the start of each sprint the team does a **sprint planning meeting**. The whole team finalizes the **Sprint Goal**. Sprint Goal is what everyone wants accomplished at the end of the sprint.

6. **Scrum board**: Agile believes in making work visible to everyone. The most common way is to create a Scrum Board. A Scrum Board has 3 columns, named Do, Doing, Done. Tasks are moved from left to right on the board based on their stage in the process.
7. **Burn down chart**: Another way of making work visible is through a burndown chart which plots the targeted points remaining in the sprint at the end of each day in a sprint. The ideal situation at the end of each sprint should be zero points left uncompleted.
8. **Daily standup / daily SCRUM**: Each day at the same time the Scrum Master meets the team and asks 3 questions:
    - What did you do yesterday to help the team finish the Sprint?
    - What will you do today to help the team finish the Sprint?
    - Is there any obstacle blocking you or the team from achieving the Sprint Goal?

    This meeting should not take more than 15 minutes and ideally people should stand and do this meeting if it is being done physically.
9. **Sprint review or sprint demo**: This is the meeting in which the final output of the sprint is presented. Any stakeholders involved like management, or the customers can also join this meeting. Only completed features or products should be presented.
10. **Sprint retrospective**: After the Sprint Demo the team should sit and analyze what went right in the Sprint, what could have gone better and what can be improved in the next Sprint. By the end of the Sprint Retrospective the Scrum Master should agree on the process improvement that the team will implement in the next Sprint.

Thus, we see that SCRUM is a specialized project management technique. SCRUM has become very popular and lots of startups and companies around the world use it.

Introduction to analytics

These days, '**data is the new oil**' has become a very famous line. Data scientists are in huge demand. Most people will tell you that you need to learn data science or AI/ML to understand data. Once you understand data only then can you scale and grow your startup's demand. I was under this impression till I read ***Lean Startup*** and a few other books.

Figure 2.11: Introduction to Analytics

What I learned was that analytics is about getting feedback from the market and not about data science. Data science may be required behind the scenes, but a startup founder should understand that analytics is more about data visualization and knowing the direction of action than complex mathematics.

Analytics is about deciding which metric will become the **primary metric** or the **North Star Metric** for the business and which **3 to 5 other**

metrics will become the secondary metrics for the business. Having many metrics is not useful as that only adds to analysis paralysis.

***Figure 2.12**: North Star Metric*

North Star Metric is the one metric that matters most to the startup. It is the guide for the whole company. When I was in Paytm (India's biggest startup in 2020) the whole company had one north star metric. That metric for Paytm during that time was **Gross Merchandise Value (GMV)**. Whenever someone paid anything using Paytm the amount was tracked as GMV. This enabled every team in the company to know its contribution very transparently. North star metric needs to be an actionable metric which clearly guides everyone in the company in the same direction.

Moreover, effort should be made to not rely on **vanity metrics**. Vanity metrics are metrics which look good to show to others but do not provide any actionable insights. For example, followers on social media generally become a vanity metric if the followers are not actively engaged.

Analytics should generally focus on the following types of metrics:

- Acquisition metrics
- Engagement metrics

- Retention metrics
- Virality metrics
- Monetization metrics

These metrics can be easily visualized and understood through the concept of a **funnel**. At the top of the funnel the acquisition metrics help us to understand if we are acquiring customers properly or not (refer to *Figure 2.13*):

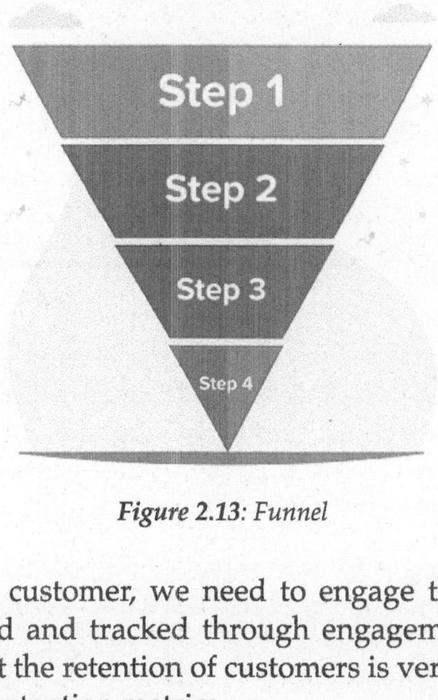

***Figure 2.13**: Funnel*

After acquiring a customer, we need to engage this customer. This can be understood and tracked through engagement metrics. For a successful product the retention of customers is very important. Thus, next we track the retention metrics.

If the customer is retained and is happy the customer will generally promote the product to others. Thus, next we should track the virality metrics. We need to track how many other customers each customer brings.

Finally, we need to track the monetization metrics. We need to track the revenue related metrics so that we achieve profitability at the earliest. Thus, we see that analytics act as eyes and ears to a startup. Analytics enable decision makers to act in the best interest of the startup.

Funnels

Analytics become easy to understand using funnels. Funnels help to understand the whole customer journey. Basically, funnels are created visually when we have multiple steps in any process and the number of people in every subsequent step reduces (refer to *Figure 2.14*):

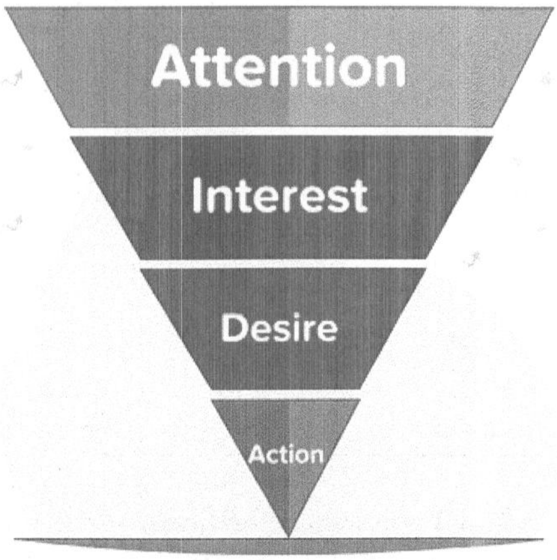

Figure 2.14: *AIDA Funnel*

I will be introducing you to two well-known types of funnels. The first one is the **AIDA funnel**. AIDA is an acronym that stands for **Attention | Interest | Desire | Action**. AIDA funnel has these 4 steps. AIDA funnel is useful in designing marketing campaigns and sales strategies:

1. The first step is to grab the attention of people. In this digital age everyone is super busy. We need something which grabs the attention of the public.

2. The next step is grabbing the interest of the customer. The customer will be interested if you tell them the benefits of the product. Generally, the number of people interested in your offering will be less than the people whose attention you had grabbed. Thus, a funnel shape is formed where each step has less people than the previous step.

3. The next step is to create a desire in the customer. To create desire, you need to create a positive emotion in the customer's mind.

4. Finally, we want the customer to take the action we want. Generally, in sales the action is the act of closing the sales.

A good example of an AIDA funnel can be seen in YouTube video-based e-commerce. When the user sees her YouTube feed, she sees lots of videos. One of those videos may grab her attention. The user will see the video cover and if interested she will start playing the video. If the user desires the product shown in the video, she will click on the link displayed on the video. Finally, the user will purchase the product through that link if she is convinced that the product is right for her.

Thus, a startup needs to master AIDA funnel if they want to sell their products online. There are other types of funnels also. One such funnel is the **'Pirate Funnel'**. The pirate funnel defines pirate metrics, and it was coined by the famous investor Dave McClure (who currently follows me on Twitter). It is also known as the AARRR framework (refer to *Figure 2.15*):

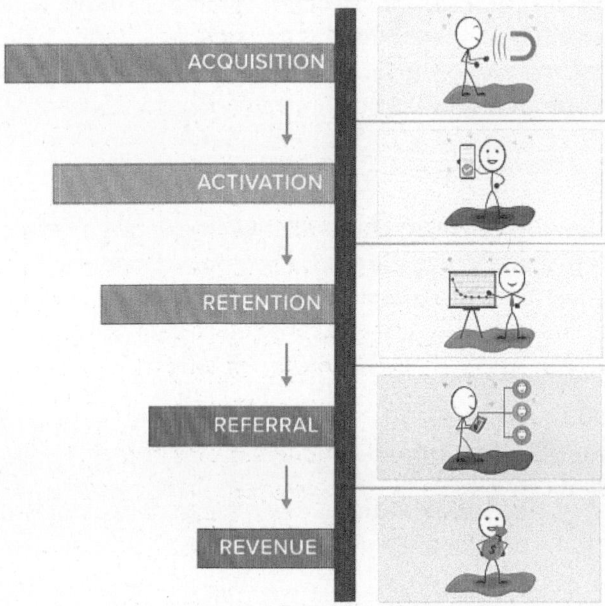

***Figure 2.15**: Pirate funnel*

The funnel has five steps, and the following is the focus area in each step:

1. **Acquisition:** Where are customers coming from?
2. **Activation:** How to turn acquired customers into active customers?
3. **Retention:** How to make active customers come back?
4. **Referral:** How to get customers to recommend your product?
5. **Revenue:** How to turn customers into paying customers?

Take the example of a startup which sells mobile messenger application.

The first metric the startup will need to track will be the customers who are being acquired that is, the number of downloads.

The second metric which needs to be tracked is the number of customers who are active. Customers who sent at least 1 message need to be tracked for that. So, we need to define when a user is considered active. Once we arrive at that definition, **Daily Active Users (DAU)** will be a good metric to track that.

The third metric will be the number of users who are being retained. For this we generally need to track if customers are coming back. We can track the percentage of customers who come back after 1 month, 2 months, 3 months and so on. This technique is also called **cohort analysis**. For an app like WhatsApp this percentage will be very high even after 6 months.

The fourth metric to track will be the virality coefficient. Virality coefficient tells how many new customers each existing customer is bringing. The more the referrals the faster the app will become popular. A good virality coefficient is 2. It means that each customer brings 2 new customers.

The fifth metric is revenue. Any startup needs money to run. Thus, revenue is a very important metric to track. A good way to measure revenue is the monthly run rate of revenue.

Thus, we see that the pirate funnel is a very important tool in understanding the customer lifecycle and growth of the product analytics.

Product management

The most important thing a startup does for the external world is to create a great product. To create a great product, we need to first understand the meaning of the product.

A product is any good, service, or information that can be offered to a market to satisfy a want or need.

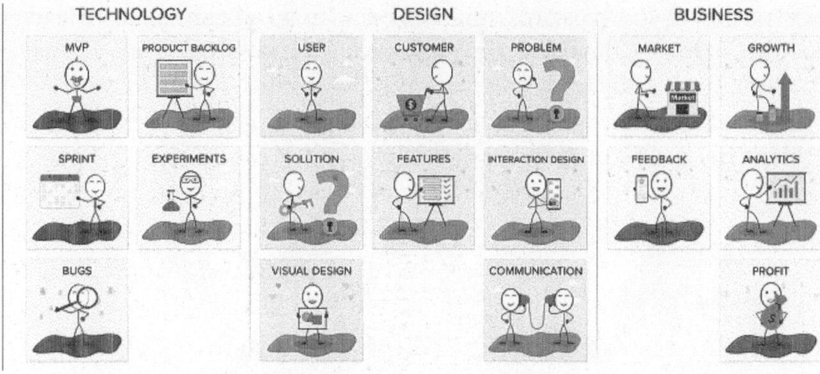

***Figure 2.16:** Product Management Canvas*

Thus, we see that a product can be a good, service, or even an intangible things like information. Gone are the days when products meant only physical products. Today, a product includes services or even information. In fact, with the advent of the internet, digital information-based products have grown rapidly.

Generally, in a big startup, the product manager has a key role in building a product. I am sharing the key focus areas of a product manager. In a small, bootstrapped startup generally, one or more founders perform the role of a product manager. Even in a Unicorn startup (startup having valuation of USD 1 billion or above), founders need to be deeply involved in product management. *Vijay Shekhar Sharma,* the founder of Paytm has been successful because of his deep expertise in product management even though Paytm has a lot of senior product managers.

Over the years, I have researched a lot on the role of product managers and built a visual tool to introduce product management. I have named this visual tool **'Product Management Canvas'**. I have got this vetted from *Deepak Abbot* who was head of product at Paytm and some other very senior product folks.

The creation of a good product starts with understanding the **user**. The user is the individual who uses the product. Next, we need to understand the **customer**. The customer is the one who pays the money to use the product. Sometimes the user and the customer are the same person. Many times, though the user and the customer are different.

Take the case of kid's education products. Generally, the customer is the parent, and the user is the child. The user and customer are almost always different in the case of **Business to Business (B2B)** products.

The next step is to investigate the real **problems** being faced by the user and the customer. The real problems are generally different from the problems stated explicitly by users and customers. As an entrepreneur or the product manager, you need to understand the context and true depth of the problem (refer to *Figure 2.17*):

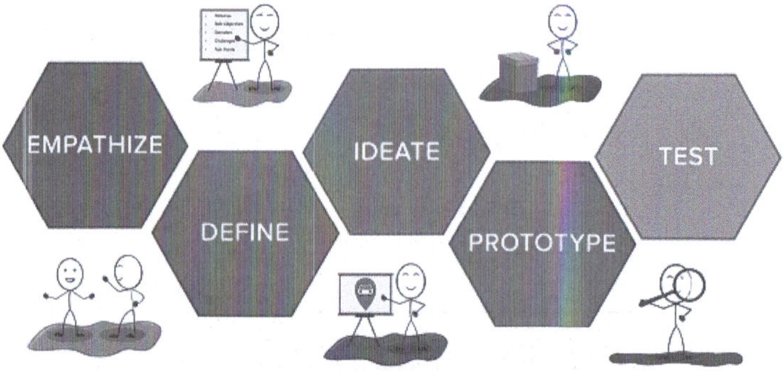

***Figure 2.17**: Design thinking*

I find **design thinking** a particularly good way to find real problems. Design thinking tells us to empathize with the user and the customer to truly understand the problem from their perspective before building a solution. It also says that multiple solutions should be ideated, prototyped and tested on the users for feedback. Sometimes after following the design thinking process, you may conclude that the original understanding of the problem was incorrect, and the true problem is something else.

You should be able to define the different types of users who will use your product. These can be represented in the form of **user personas**. User personas are fictional indicative users who will use your product. Defining user personas makes it easy to develop and discuss product features. You should ideally talk to many potential users before defining your final user personas.

Once personas are finalized you need to understand the value proposition of your product for the customer. The customer buys the product to get value. You need to define the jobs which customers want to get completed with your product. You also need to define the pain points for the customers and areas where you can provide a feeling of satisfaction or gain to the customers.

Then you need to define features which act as job providers, pain relievers and gain creators for the customers. A good tool to understand these in more detail is **'value proposition canvas'** which is described in more detail in the book, ***Value Proposition Design***.

Next, you need to create a **list of features** that should be there in the product. This forms the road map of product development. Creating various features takes time and thus you would not be able to develop all features in one go. A startup is generally always starved of resources and thus you will need to prioritize your features. A general best practice is to create a list of all features and prioritize them according to the order in which you want to develop them. This prioritized list of features to be developed is called the **product backlog**.

Generally, these days the products are developed by following the agile methodology. There are multiple ways of working according to agile methodology but generally, the most famous approach is **SCRUM**. In SCRUM you do the work in **sprints**. Sprints are fixed time periods in which a team aims to complete some preselected tasks. Generally, the goal of a sprint is to complete a few shippable features. Some companies use 1-week sprints while others may use up to 4-week sprints. The team is free to select its own sprint time. The only constraint imposed is that the time selected should be the same in each sprint. Thus, if you do weekly sprints you need to always follow weekly sprints. If you follow 2-week sprints, then always follow 2-week sprints.

Another thing to keep in mind is that you should try to go to the market in the shortest time possible. In the internet age, things are always changing in the market and thus you cannot wait for months or years to complete finished products. The Lean Startup methodology tells us that we should start by creating a **minimum viable product (MVP)**. A minimum viable product is a product with the smallest possible feature set that you can release in the market. The aim of releasing the product is to go to the real market with actual customers and users to learn more about them. The focus is on getting the taste of the real market at an early stage so that any feedback can be incorporated at the earliest.

As per *Eric Ries*, author of the famous book ***The Lean Startup***, any startup should launch MVP in a few months and then try to add features based on the BUILD | MEASURE | LEARN loop. He says that we should build features in sprints and then launch the updated product in the market. This is especially easy in the case of digital products like mobile apps and websites. We should try to collect usage data and user feedback and then learn how users are using the product in real life. Based on the usage pattern and feedback we should reprioritize the product backlog before each sprint. **If we follow this process our product will always be built according to the user's needs.**

Great products give a great user experience (UX). We should focus on designing the product in a way that the product provides a great user experience. Steve Jobs was a great proponent of user experience in Apple products. We can also give a great user experience if we focus on interaction design while designing and building our products. Once we finish with interaction design, we should focus on creating the best visual design possible for the product.

A good user interface is necessary for providing a great user experience. Thus, the user interface should be designed with the utmost care and the best practices of interaction design and visual design should be followed wherever possible.

Finally, a product manager must focus on business related aspects like marketing, analytics, revenue and profit.

This is the broad recipe to create great products, especially digital products. Most Silicon Valley companies and new-age startups across the world use some form of this process to create great products.

Market size

Startup investors want to invest in a startup that can grow 100x in the next 5 years. You need to have the potential to win in a big market in the next few years. Thus, you need to calculate the market size for your startup and clearly tell the following to investors:

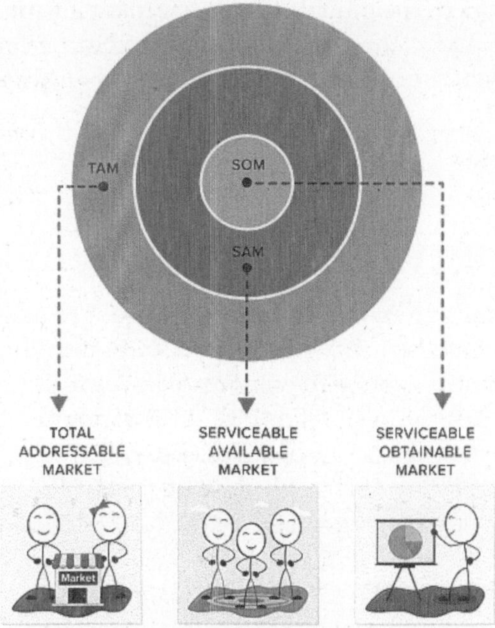

Figure 2.18: Market size

- **Total Addressable Market (TAM)**: Total market demand for the product

  For example: For a global EdTech startup focusing on school education the total addressable market is around 2 billion kids. Say if the product is a mobile game for kids and the estimated average potential price per download is USD 5 then the total TAM will be 2 billion x USD 5 = USD 10 billion dollars.

- **Serviceable Available Market (SAM)**: Total market of the product that can be reached practically.

  For example: For a global EdTech startup focusing on school education the SAM will be based on kids who have access to the internet or some offline digital medium. If a kid is not having any digital access, then the EdTech company cannot practically reach the kid. This figure will be smaller than TAM. So if say 1 billion kids have digital access globally and they can be sold a USD 5 app than the SAM will be 1 billion x USD 5 = USD 5 billion.

- **Serviceable Obtainable Market (SOM)**: Total portion of SAM that can be captured after competition from competitors

For example: For the global EdTech company this may be just 30% of the total SAM as there may be multiple competitors. So the SOM in this case will be USD 1.5 billion on SAM of USD 5 billion.

Investors generally would not invest if you do not share TAM, SAM and SOM or if their values are small.

Technology adoption life cycle

The market never accepts a product at one go. The market will have various types of customers who will accept the product as per their own thinking process and convenience. Years ago, I bumped into this concept called **Technology Adoption Life Cycle** which introduced me to how the market really behaves. Here, I will give you a brief introduction to it.

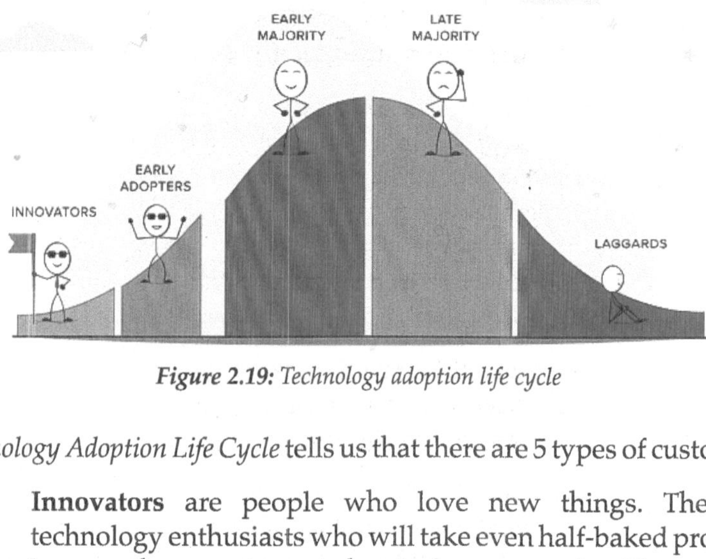

***Figure 2.19:** Technology adoption life cycle*

Technology Adoption Life Cycle tells us that there are 5 types of customers:

- **Innovators** are people who love new things. They are technology enthusiasts who will take even half-baked products because they want to get ahead of everyone else. These people are few and will be the first users of any technically advanced product. For example, the first people who purchased mobile phones were of this category.
- The second group of customers are the **Early Adopters**. These people are visionaries who can foresee how a new product will enhance their productivity or prestige. They have creativity to foresee the early uses of the product in their personal or professional life. These people are a very important set of customers for a startup. The people who started using mobile

phones in the 1990s for their early benefits were from this category.

- Between the second and third group of customers is a gap or **chasm**. This chasm tells us that the behavior of the first two groups of customers is very different from the rest of the three groups of customers. The first two groups of customers that is the innovators and early adopters represent the early market. The third, fourth and fifth group of customers represent the mainstream market.
- The third group of customers are called **Early Majority**. These people are practical and want to solve a problem using this product as the solution. They want the evidence of the product working effectively before purchasing it. They will look for the experience of early adopters before making the decision. People who purchased mobile phones in the early 2000s were from this category.
- The fourth group of customers are called **Late Majority**. These are conservative in their decisions. They prefer to wait until the technology has become a standard. These are the people who do not like to take risks and do not want to change their habits. The people who only purchased mobile phones when many people had them will fall into this category.
- The fifth group of customers are the **Laggards**. These are sceptics who will not buy even when most people have bought similar products. Focusing on these people is a waste of time for the startup. These customers prefer the status quo. People who have not bought mobile phones till now fall into this category.

Thus, we see that technology adoption life cycle provides us a model to understand the different types of customers in the market and how they will adopt our products. A startup needs to be aware of this model to focus resources on the right type of customers at the right stage.

Digital business models

Digital businesses have been growing the world over. All offline businesses also want to move online. The problem is that an online business is not just an offline business with a website or an app. A successful digital business demands a clear understanding of digital business models and the digital way of working.

Figure 2.20: Digital Business Models

Digital businesses can be of many types but generally the world over digital business models fall into 6 broad categories:

- Ads
- Subscriptions
- Paid downloads
- Freemium
- E-commerce
- Uber for X

Ads

Most early internet businesses were ad supported and Google's ad solutions really helped such businesses. The reason was that initially, the internet did not have online payments at scale. Ads are still a big business model for media related businesses. Ad supported business is viable only when you can garner an extremely large audience for your content. Once you have a large audience for your online content you can monetize it through ads.

Ads from ad networks can be shown for money or ads can be procured directly from advertisers. Generally, direct procurement is possible only for big advertisers and initially, most businesses try to source ads from ad networks. Google runs the most prominent ad network.

Subscriptions

Many online businesses are now shifting to subscription-based business models. Media businesses are especially exploring subscriptions in a big way. I have been advising a big media company in India over the years for their digital business and I have seen that subscriptions are a viable way to run an online content business. Subscriptions can also be explored in areas like gaming, EdTech, FinTech etc. Amazon even allows you to subscribe for items like detergent powder!

Software as a Service (SaaS) is a big business these days. Subscriptions are one of the best business models and offer good long-term revenue potential once customers start liking the product.

Paid downloads

Paid downloads is a popular business model in mobile applications and games business. The Apple App Store offers rich opportunities to monetize app downloads. Google Play is also now catching up with the Apple App Store. In the initial days of the internet most people did not want to pay for apps, but this is now changing. People have become more habitual in paying for online apps now.

Freemium

Many customers are initially apprehensive in downloading paid apps or content. A good way to break the ice with such customers is to offer freemium content. Freemium content means that you offer a part of the product free and then the user must pay for getting access to the rest of the product. Mobile games use the Freemium business model extensively. Media companies these days use freemium extensively.

E-Commerce

E-Commerce is one of the earliest digital business models. Amazon has been there practically since the start of the consumer internet. E-Commerce has become big over the years and most countries now have entrenched big E-Commerce players. A big problem in E-Commerce is logistics cost and complexity. Amazon and many other companies also offer their platforms for selling goods to 3rd party merchants. This has also become a viable option for selling E-Commerce stuff in many categories.

Uber for X

Ever since Uber succeeded many online businesses have started taking inspiration from Uber in various offline business categories. 'Urban Company' in India is one such startup that has been providing high-quality repairing and maintenance services for homes and offices. In this business model, the main activity is done offline but the app or website acts as an interface between the offline service provider and the customer. The app provider also supports offline service providers through various helpful services. The total user experience is better than pure offline vendors and thus this business model is a win-win for all concerned if executed properly.

The choice of any of the above business models depends on your offering in the market and careful business analysis. Generally, subscription is the most profitable business model as it offers regular money. Also, you can mix and match various business models.

A good example is Zoho which offers its software products as a subscription service and allows free usage of some products up to certain limits. Thus, this application uses subscriptions in conjunction with the Freemium business model. Amazon allows you to subscribe to E-Commerce products. Amazon Prime is also a good example of mixed business models. Media companies these days mix ads, subscriptions, and freemium business models. Some of them also combine E-Commerce in their offerings.

Thus, any startup should not go by fixed notions of business models. It should try to understand the various available options suitable for its offerings and try to innovate within available choices. Google was a business that became super successful due to its highly innovative business model initially. Google was able to give customers free search engine and in parallel became the biggest ads company in the world. It was able to create such a big competitive advantage through its business model that no company has been able to challenge it in its core offering till now.

What is product market fit?

Every startup dreams of becoming famous and successful. A significant milestone in this journey is achieving **'product market fit'**. Product market fit is one of those terms which may mean different things to different people. Many industry experts define it differently. Yet broadly it means that the startup has found its way in the market and from hereon it will find it easier to grow.

Product market fit is generally defined as the stage in which the startup creates a product that is being pulled by the market at such a rapid pace that the startup has a difficult time fulfilling demand. At this point, the product starts resonating with the customer (refer to *Figure 2.2*):

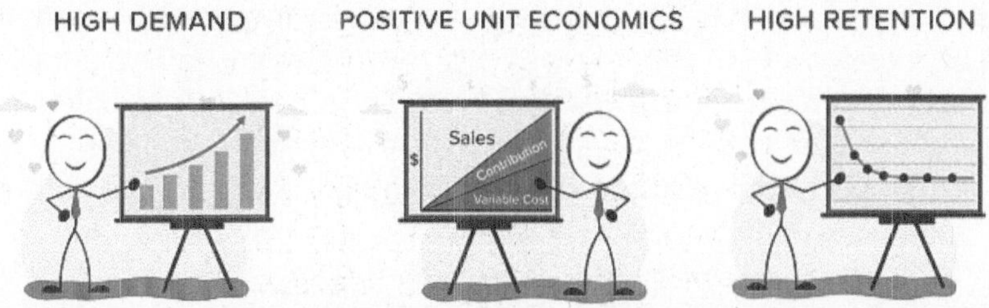

***Figure 2.21**: Product market fit*

Before achieving the product market fit generally, the startup has a hard time pushing the product in the market. One or more issues are there which stop the startup from being able to sell the product at a rapid pace. Once the startup finds the sweet spot in the market through multiple iterations in the product or through changes in the market dynamics the startup suddenly sees a spurt in demand. At this point, the startup starts to see so much demand that the startup finds it hard to match the supply.

I have been part of Paytm (India's highest valued startup in 2019 and 2020), which achieved product market fit in 2016. At that time the Indian government started promoting digital payments to curb black money in India and suddenly people started using digital payments. Many of them started liking the convenience of Paytm's payment products and Paytm saw 100x growth in registered users within a few years. In fact, by 2020 Paytm had more downloads than the population of the USA which is the third most populous country in the world!

We all have seen this with Uber, Facebook, WhatsApp, etc., in the past. I personally remember how difficult it was to travel outside the home city before Uber. Even in my home city, Uber did add a lot of convenience.

After studying the product market fit from various angles and personally observing it in Paytm, I would like to define it as a point in a startup's lifecycle when there are 3 things going for a startup:

- High demand
- High customer retention
- Positive unit economics

High demand

High demand means that the startup starts seeing a lot of demand from the customers in the market. This may be due to updates in the product or changes in the market or both. The startup should focus on creating the best user experience and customer satisfaction from the day it introduces the **Minimum Viable Product (MVP)** in the market. Every iteration of the product should bring a startup closer to this goal.

High customer retention

High customer retention should also be a focus area for every startup. If the customer retention is low, then fulfilling growth would be like pouring water in a leaking bucket. If you want the bucket to fill up, then you must stop leakage. Similarly, a good startup tries to minimize customer usage drop at every interaction point.

Customer retention can easily be measured through **cohort analysis**. If the customers who start their journey on any given day keep coming back to use the product even after many weeks or months have passed, then we can say that the startup has a sticky product, and it has high retention.

If you plot a graph of the percentage of people coming back after every week or month, you can analyze the retention graphically. In the case of good product retention, the graph falls initially a bit but then stabilizes and flattens out. Good companies like Uber and Paytm have people coming back again and again to use their products.

Positive unit economics

I believe that a startup should be able to recover its variable cost on each transaction to reach the milestone of the product market fit. Startups need to spend heavily on product development and marketing and thus the fixed cost of startups is quite high. These costs may be recovered in multiple years. Also, product market fit is the starting point of the high demand phase. Recovering full fixed costs will take time.

For a startup to achieve product market fit, transactions with the customer should be able to recover the variable costs involved. Otherwise, if the startup is losing money on every transaction, then doing more transactions overall will just increase the losses at a very high rate. On the other hand, if the variable costs are being recovered fully then every transaction will bring the company closer to overall profit. **Beyond a certain scale of transactions, the startup will turn profitable.**

Product market fit is a very important milestone in a startup's journey from multiple points of view. Till this point, the startup would be iterating the product to find the sweet spot in the market. Beyond this point, the focus will be to retain this sweet spot and accelerate growth.

The **Venture Capitalists (VCs)** also focuses a lot on the startup having product market fit before funding it. If the startup has not reached the sweet spot in the market where it can grow rapidly the venture capitalists are generally apprehensive about investing in that startup. Thus, reaching the product market fit becomes critical in order to attract big VCs. Consequently, every startup needs to focus on achieving product market fit as soon as possible.

When should your startup pivot?

Sometimes a startup works hard, iterates a lot of times but still cannot reach the product market fit. In that case the startup needs to **Pivot**. Pivot as a term has been made popular by *Eric Ries* in his book ***The Lean Startup***. According to him, a pivot is a change in strategy without a change in vision (refer to *Figure* 2.22):

Figure 2.22: *When should your startup pivot?*

According to *Eric Ries,* pivots are necessary because even though the destination remains the same, due to heavy obstacles in the path ahead we must change the path to the destination. We must find an alternative path to the destination which is easier to travel on.

If you do lots of experiments with different aspects of your product but are unable to get to the product market fit, then it is the clearest sign that you need to pivot (refer to *Figure 2.23*):

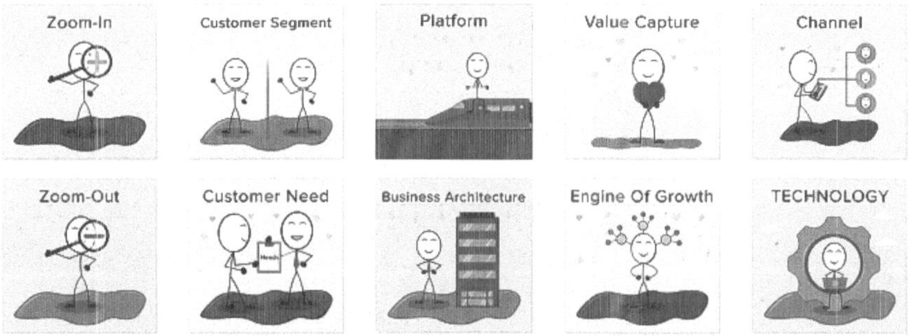

Figure 2.23: *Types of pivot*

Eric Ries has described 10 types of pivots in his book **The Lean Startup**. They have been summarized here:

- **Zoom-in pivot:** What was previously considered a single feature in the whole product now becomes the whole product. Instagram is a famous example of this type of pivot.
- **Zoom-out pivot:** This is the reverse of the Zoom-in pivot. What was previously considered the whole product, becomes the single feature of a much larger product.
- **Customer segment pivot:** The product may prove popular but not with the user segment that was initially targeted. Thus, the targeted customer segment is changed in this kind of pivot.
- **Customer need pivot:** Startup finds that the customer has a problem that's worth solving more than the current customer problem it is trying to solve.
- **Platform pivot:** This is when you pivot from making applications on a platform to being the platform itself or vice versa.
- **Business architecture pivot:** This is when you change from high margin, low volume product to low margin, high volume product or vice versa.

- **Value capture pivot:** Changing the way your business captures value from the customer.
- **Engine of growth pivot:** *Eric Ries* talks about 3 engines of growth:
    - Viral engine of growth
    - Sticky engine of growth
    - Paid engine of growth

  In this type of pivot, he refers to the change in the engine of growth of the product from one type to another.
- **Channel pivot:** Same product but different channel. Changing sales or distribution channels for greater effectiveness.
- **Technology pivot:** A company provides the same solution by using a completely different technology. A good example is Netflix which shifted from renting DVDs to online streaming of movies over the internet.

Thus, when you feel that you cannot reach product market fit under any circumstances, you need to start thinking about pivoting. Pivoting is an essential tool in the startup's arsenal. It helps the startup, start again with the same vision but a different strategy with renewed vigor.

Growth profit fit

The third phase in product development as per Startup Canvas is 'Growth Profit Fit'. In the first phase we try to find the **problem solution fit**. In the second phase we try to find the **product market fit**. Once we achieve the product market fit, we can find large pools of capital. Venture capitalists are generally interested in funding startups which have achieved product market fit.

***Figure 2.24:** Growth profit fit*

Thus, the third phase for a startup with respect to product development is **growth profit fit**. In this phase the startup starts focusing whole heartedly on growth. Since the startup has the product market fit the aim is to reach the whole of the market and capture it.

For example, if a food startup has found the product market fit in one city, after raising large pools of capital it may look to expand across the country. For achieving fast growth, the startup generally needs to scale rapidly. Large pools of capital enable a startup to do so.

Due to burning large pools of money on growth generally a startup goes into massive losses at this stage. The investors are okay with that as they know that at a certain large scale the startup will eventually turn profitable. In fact, after startups achieve really large scale they can become super profitable. Amazon is a good example of this.

Engines of growth for a startup

Every startup wants to grow fast. Fast growth cannot happen with just plain vanilla marketing. Startups must find the growth engine that will help it deliver its products well. Marketing techniques will be determined by the growth engine chosen by the startup. A startup can even choose multiple growth engines.

The following are the 3 engines of growth mentioned by *Eric Ries* in his famous book **The Lean Startup**:

- Viral
- Sticky
- Paid

***Figure 2.25**: Engines of growth for a startup*

Viral engine of growth

We all know about the Coronavirus. Even though COVID has ravaged the world I am in awe of COVID when studying virality. It is a big force, and we have all have been at the receiving end of it, during the pandemic. **Virality refers to the process where 1 person brings 1 or more people to the product.**

If 1 person brings 2 others and 2 bring 4 others, your product can grow very rapidly. There is no way for the users to defend themselves from product virus if the product is truly viral.

This happened with COVID pandemic, and this force was the reason WhatsApp became number 1 chat app in India in spite of its competitors using Bollywood celebrities to promote themselves. WhatsApp had very high word of mouth while the competitors had practically none.

Virality Coefficient = invitations sent per user X conversion rate (%)

Virality is the reason why Facebook, Instagram or Twitter became hits. The thing a startup has to do to make the product viral is to make the virality coefficient more than 1. If 1 person brings more than 1 person, then the product will grow exponentially. If 1 person brings only 1 person, the growth will still be there, but it will be slower. If a user does not bring at least one more user, then the product will not be used widely, and will not grow how its founders intended it to grow.

Sticky engine of growth

Sticky engine of growth refers to the stickiness of the user to the product. A good example is Uber. I first used Uber in San Francisco in 2015. Ever since that time I have been using Uber. The more a user uses a product the more they will spend on that product and more will they promote a product people around, indirectly.

When I used Uber for my commute outside my home city and even in my home city while going to office sometimes many others would also have been motivated to use Uber after witnessing me use it. Thus, my loyalty indirectly helped in the growth of Uber.

Paid engine of growth

Paid engine of growth refers to the ability of a startup to charge a large sum of money for the product so that it can spend money to acquire even more users. Byju's (biggest EdTech startup in India in 2022) is a great example of a paid engine of growth. Their product costs ₹ 30,000-40,000 generally in turn, leading them to having high margins. They can use this high margin to give high sales commissions and spend on paid ads in Cricket matches and TV channels.

A startup like WhatsApp would not have been successful if it used the paid engine of growth instead of the viral engine of growth. Thus, a startup needs to understand which product will be able to use which engine of growth.

Some startups use multiple engines of growth. Paytm is a good example. It uses all 3 engines of growth. Paytm is not as viral as WhatsApp, but it is quite viral as a product. During COVID I asked my local shopkeeper to receive payments through Paytm as we were not going to the bank and thus were short on cash in the COVID lockdown days. Thus, Paytm's users put pressure on shopkeepers and their friends to use Paytm.

Let us take Paytm as an example for it is quite addictive. Once somebody starts using this digital banking app to pay bills, they continue using the same for a very long time. In fact, using online payment methods become easier for it as it provides multiple services once one becomes regular customer.

This app uses a paid engine of growth also. Paytm sponsors cricket matches extensively and has a sales force for getting new merchants. It however does not have as high a margin as Byju's but has raised a lot of capital and is able to use this engine of growth also.

Thus, a startup should not blindly buy Google Ads or Facebook Ads for growth. It should focus on finding the right engines of growth and construct a marketing strategy around that keeping the right engines of growth at the core. Engines of growth chosen would also depend on the budget of the startup.

Growth hacking

Every startup wants to grow as fast as possible. In this digital age there are lots of ways to reach customers, but every potential customer has lots of competitive options. Thus, startups find it difficult to grow.

Growth hacking is a term often used to describe the techniques which can help a startup to grow fast. In the digital age growth techniques are a combination of marketing and coding.

Figure 2.26*: Growth hacking*

Some of the most popular techniques for growth hacking are:

- **Search Engine Optimization (SEO):** Gaining traction on search engines, gives free traffic to your website. Moreover, becoming popular through Google's searches gives you a lot of free traffic. Experts have studied Google's search engine behavior and devised various strategies for making a website popular. Search Engine Optimization refers to these techniques which, when used can help you grow your website traffic.

- **Blogs:** Another popular technique to promote your website is to write regular blogs. People on the internet are searching for knowledge and blogs are a popular way to share that knowledge.

- **Social Media Marketing (SMM):** These days social media is very popular. People spend hours every day on it. Creating social media content and sharing it, is a good way of promoting your products and reaching your target audience.

- **Digital ads:** Ads on search engines and social media are a useful way of promoting your products. Creating content and sharing that on your website and social media takes time and effort. Ads provide a convenient way to get growth although the startup needs to pay for them. Many startups spend heavily on Google Ads and Facebook Ads to gain traction.

- **Email marketing:** Sending emailers and newsletters are also a great way of building a loyal audience. Sending daily, weekly, fortnightly, or monthly newsletters is a growth technique used by many companies. Various companies have also started sending emailers based on the user's journey on their digital products. Hence, they send an email at various times to people according to the context of usage of their mobile or web applications.

- **Content marketing:** Content marketing refers to the creation of content that can be distributed on the internet for free. This helps to get customer data as the potential customers must give their contact details to download this content. Additionally, this creates goodwill on the internet and establishes thought leadership.
- **PR:** Press releases and coverage in the press are very important sources of building goodwill. It may not help to sell directly in this age of digital media, but it does create goodwill for the startup. *Richard Branson* has used PR as a big tool in popularizing his Virgin brand all over the world.
- **Offline Ads:** Old style offline ads can also be used to popularize certain products. Offline ads in newspapers or hoardings still give a sense of credibility to the startup.
- **Viral Features:** Creating virality through product is the best growth hack. It involves designing and coding a feature in a way that promotes natural virality. Many games allow social media sharing. Some apps and games allow multiplayer features. All these are good examples of creating viral features for growth.
- **Community building:** Building an online community is also a good growth hack. Online communities when combined with few offline events in turn, create stronger communities. Many companies like Amazon, Microsoft and Google use these for their software developer related products.
- **Sales:** Traditional sales teams are a good way to increase traction. Sales teams focused on selling products can bring excellent results.

Profit

Profit is the main goal, for which the startup exists. Entrepreneurs would like to profit from day one however most startups take a considerable amount of time to become profitable. The reason this time is required and important is because one needs scale along with good revenue and control over costs.

Whenever a business sells a product, a part of the cost is associated directly with production and sales. This is called a **variable cost**. Variable costs change directly in proportion to the change in production or sales.

Figure 2.27: Profit

The costs which do not change with the level of production or sales are called **fixed costs**. These are generally the cost of human resources, cost of office rental, overhead costs and so on.

To create a profitable business, you need your revenue to be more than your expenditure. At a smaller scale, the startup is initially at a loss because the fixed costs start at a very high level. Every sale recovers only a part of the fixed cost. Thus, you need sales to be at a certain scale to recover all the fixed costs. The point where all the fixed costs and variable costs are recovered that is, all the costs are recovered is called **break-even point** (refer to *Figure 2.28*):

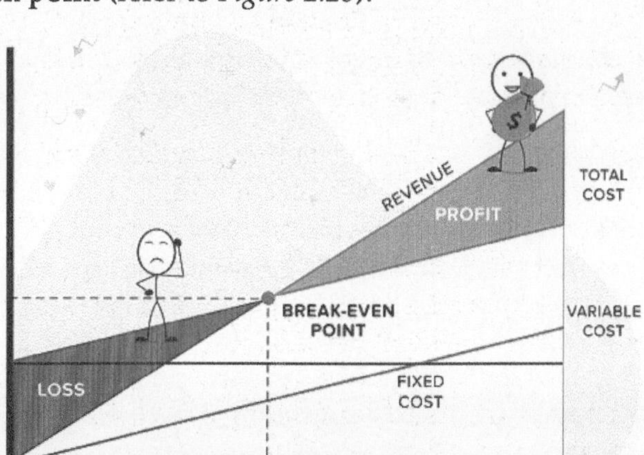

Figure 2.28: Revenue and cost curves

Beyond break-even point every sale adds to the profit of the startup.

Numerous people are curious about why the investors invest in loss making startups. The reason generally is that the startup has achieved product market fit with positive unit economics. Positive unit economics means that every time the product is sold the variable cost is less than the revenue. Thus, the **contribution profit** (revenue – variable cost) is in each sale.

Thus, the investors know that putting more money in the startup will help the startup grow and reach a scale at which it will be able to fully recover fixed costs and become profitable. Product market fit gives the assurance that the startup will be able to grow with increasing contribution profit with every sale.

Once the profitability is reached, if the startup continues to grow at a fast pace, then it starts earning increased profits. Amazon is a good example of such a phenomenon.

Conclusion

In this chapter we learned a lot about products. We learned how to find a big problem to solve and how to find a scalable solution to it. We also learned about product management, analytics, and funnels. We discussed product market fit, pivots, and growth hacking. Finally, we learned about contribution profit and profitability in general.

Products are the reason for a startup's existence. Creating and iterating the products is the focus area for any startup. This chapter has helped you in this endeavor. Every successful product is created by a team of human beings who had a hand in its success.

In the next chapter, we will learn about managing human resources for a startup.

Join our book's Discord space

Join the book's Discord Workspace for Latest updates, Offers, Tech happenings around the world, New Release and Sessions with the Authors:

https://discord.bpbonline.com

CHAPTER 3
People

Introduction

Recruiting and managing people is a very important area for a startup founder. We see many talented people who fail to run a successful startup due to their lack of management skills despite them being domain experts. The most important thing people should learn from Paytm is the importance of a team in building a Unicorn startup. *Vijay Shekhar Sharma,* the founder of Paytm has built a strong core team that helps him to manage this digital giant, which has contributed to its exponential growth over the last few years.

***Figure 3.1:** People*

Structure

This chapter will cover the following topics:

- Qualities of a great founder
- Finding Co-founders
- Co-founder: Legal aspects
- Core team
- How to remunerate early startup employees?
- Office versus remote work
- Human Resources: Legal aspects
- Outsourcing versus internal development
- Building a corporation

Objectives

The reader will better understand the aspects related to human resource management after reading this chapter. This chapter will give the reader an understanding of the aspects to remember while recruiting co-founders, core team and vendors. This chapter will also provide the reader with an overview of the scaling aspects of human resource management.

Qualities of a great founder

Founders are the seeds of a startup. For a startup to grow at a consistent speed it needs high-quality founders. A lot of research has been conducted on this topic and a visual tool called **Founder Canvas** has been created by me to demystify this. Most of the qualities described in Founder Canvas are present in *Mr. Vijay Shekhar Sharma*. Have also met many successful entrepreneurs and have found these to be the common traits in many of them. These traits also form the basis of a successful partnership between co-founders.

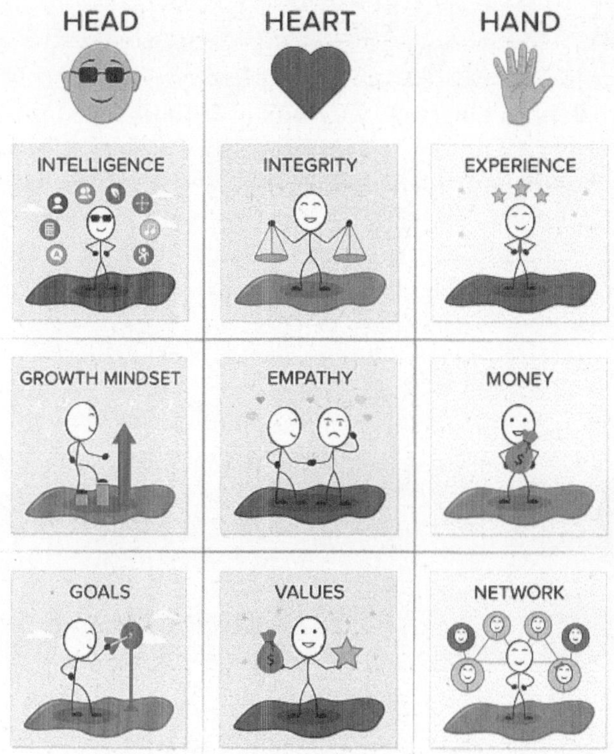

***Figure 3.2:** Founder canvas*

Thus, you can use Founder Canvas to learn how you can improve as a startup founder and who can be a good co-founder for your organization.

We can also judge a founder through 3 lenses. The 3 lenses and what they denote are:

- **Head:** Intelligence, growth mindset, and goals
- **Heart:** Integrity, empathy, and values
- **Hand:** Experience, money, and network

Head

Head is the first lens through which we can judge a founder. This lens helps us to understand the intelligence and mindset of the founder. It further has three sub-sections to it:

Intelligence

Intelligence is extremely important in order to be successful. Generally, when we talk of intelligence, we think of **Intelligence Quotient (IQ)**. In my experience IQ should never be the true measure of and the only criteria for, intelligence. In the 1980s, **'Theory of Multiple Intelligences'** was introduced by Harvard University professor, *Howard Gardner*. The theory of multiple intelligences tells us that human beings have multiple types of intelligence and that there are at least 8 types of intelligences:

- Logical intelligence
- Linguistic intelligence
- Interpersonal intelligence
- Intrapersonal intelligence
- Naturalistic intelligence
- Musical intelligence
- Kinesthetic intelligence
- Spatial intelligence

This theory was introduced in the book **Frames of Mind**. I started working with *Vijay Shekhar Sharma,* founder of Paytm in late 2017 and it was interesting to know that *Vijay* had all 8 types of intelligence. He has been one of the most successful entrepreneurs in India in the 21st century and is testament to the fact that there are certain qualities any entrepreneur should possess to be successful.

5 intelligences out of the 8 are very crucial for any entrepreneur. Ability to think logically, command over the language, great interpersonal skills, and knowing the reason behind working hard. All these are all very crucial.

An interesting intelligence as per this theory is **naturalistic intelligence**. It was introduced by *Howard Gardner* in the 1990s, many years after the introduction of this theory. It refers to the ability to see patterns in the natural world. This ability to see patterns in the natural world also helps in seeing patterns of technical change years ahead of everyone. In *Vijay's* case, he foresaw the power of digital payments in India well before others.

Growth mindset

Carol Dweck introduced 2 terms: **Growth mindset** and **Fixed mindset.** According to her, the growth mindset refers to the thinking in which an individual believes that abilities can grow with hard work. Individuals with a fixed mindset do not believe in this. They believe that abilities cannot change. They run away from difficult things.

People with a growth mindset believe in learning from mistakes. People with a fixed mindset try to find fault in others. People with a growth mindset embrace challenges while people with a fixed mindset run away from challenges. People with a growth mindset persist in face of setbacks while the ones with a fixed mindset bow down to setbacks.

A good entrepreneur needs to have a growth mindset in order to succeed. If entrepreneurs run away from challenges, they will fail in creating a successful business. Entrepreneurs must also be able to digest market feedback while being good learners. They need to be persistent despite constant setbacks.

Goals

An entrepreneur needs to be relatively clear about his or her life goals. A wavering person cannot become a successful entrepreneur. Also, if you are looking for a co-founder then your goals and the goals of the other person should match else there would be differences later which may impact a startup's work.

Heart

Heart is the second lens through which we can judge a founder. Heart gives us insight into the character of the person.

Integrity

According to *Warren Buffet,* he will not hire anyone without integrity. All successful people work only with people they trust. Thus, a successful entrepreneur needs to have integrity as otherwise employees, investors and customers will not work with him or her. Also, a co-founder needs to have integrity as if that person does not have integrity, then you will have a very bad time with that person.

Empathy

A great product can only be built by a startup if the entrepreneur has great empathy for the user. *Vijay Shekhar Sharma* has empathized with the end user and tried to solve the problems of the user. He always tries to think from the shoes of the user and analyzes whether the user can understand a feature or not. This is the reason why Paytm has hundreds of millions of downloads in India in such a short time.

Values

Values refer to the morals and constraints we impose on ourselves due to our thought of right and wrong in life. 2 people can have different values and still be successful. The only issue is that you need to be in sync in values with your co-founder. If 1 co-founder wants to grow through corrupt practices and the other does not, then there will be in-fighting in the startup at some stage. This is a major reason why startup founders should know each other for a long time before starting a startup together.

Hand

Practical strengths of the founders are the **hand** which entails the practical strengths that are necessary for a startup to create a good product and grow.

Experience

Experience in the domain in which the startup is focusing is a great advantage for the startup. A good founder should aim for domain expertise. In case a founder does not know the problem domain then sometimes it may make sense to even recruit a co-founder who has expertise in the specific domain.

Money

A founder who has money to invest in a startup is obviously a great asset to the startup. If you do not have money as a founder, try to get a co-founder who is willing to invest. Having capital from the founders is way better than having it from investors. Founders are more involved in the business and thus are more committed to it than investors.

Network

A founder who has connections in the industry will obviously find it easy to build the product and grow. If you do not have a network in the industry, try to recruit a co-founder who has the required network in the industry.

Thus, we see that a startup founder needs to have multiple traits in order to be successful. Not all people have all the traits. This is where the need for the co-founders arises. The co-founders should be selected based on these above discussed traits. Combined all the co-founders should be able to bring in all the necessary traits for a startup to be successful.

Finding co-founders

Doing everything alone for a startup founder is difficult. Thus, the need arises for a startup co-founder. Generally, a startup has 2-3 co-founders. The problem which many startups' founders face is that they do not have co-founders to do startup with. Thus, finding a co-founder becomes a challenge.

Figure 3.3: Finding Co-founders

The first thing a founder should analyze is the need for a co-founder. Generally, the latter should be able to provide some complimentary skills and invest some money into the startup. Startup founders also need to understand that once the co-founder is involved, the control of the startup will need to be shared with him or her as well. Moreover, many investors do not invest if the startup has a solo founder. One such reason could be that at times an entrepreneur is lacking in technical or sales skills and thus a co-founder is required to provide those skills.

Thus, most entrepreneurs will need to look for a co-founder. The best place to find a co-founder is your college or university. If you are a student and want to start a startup, then college or university is the best place to start searching for a co-founder. If you are doing a job and have some colleagues who are interested in being an entrepreneur, you can try finding some like-minded people as co-founders from within your workplace. Sometimes a friend or a relative can also become a good co-founder although many a times this can put a strain on your relationship later, if things do not work in your favor.

You can even find co-founders from attending startup ecosystem events. Many like-minded people attend startup ecosystem events. These events generally provide a good place to find like-minded people. Furthermore, some startup ecosystem organizations also conduct founder dating events where they call people looking for co-founders. Such events are good places to find like-minded people although you should analyze the person thoroughly before making him or her your co-founder.

However, the first point to understand is the goal of the co-founder. It needs to match your goal, as the founder. Moreover, the values of the co-founder are also extremely crucial. Generally, it is recommended that each co-founder invests equal money in the company, so that all individuals have equal skin in the game. Finding a co-founder is as critical as finding a life partner. Thus take your time, analyze the person, thoroughly before reaching a conclusion.

Co-founder: Legal aspects

Having a co-founder is one of the most critical decisions in a startup. Once you have found someone to be a co-founder then you need to take certain legal steps to safeguard yourself.

Figure 3.4: Co-Founder Legal Aspects

The first thing you need is to document the terms and conditions you negotiate with your co-founder. There should be no ambiguity in any negotiations. Such ambiguity can later cause a lot of mistrust between the partners.

If you are running your startup as a sole proprietorship, then this is a good time to consider forming a company. Else you can even form a partnership firm by having a written partnership deed between the co-founders. Consult a good **lawyer** or **Chartered Accountant (CA)** or **Certified Public Accountant (CPA)** while forming a partnership firm or company.

If the co-founder is investing equal money, then you can give equal shares to him or her. Else shares should generally be distributed in the ratio of the investment made.

Sometimes a co-founder does not invest money but acts as a working partner and gets some shares in that capacity. In that case you should not give all shares immediately and instead give those shares over a period. Generally, this is called **'founder vesting'** and the shares should generally vest over a period. 4 years is the industry standard in vesting of shares (refer to *Figure 3.5*):

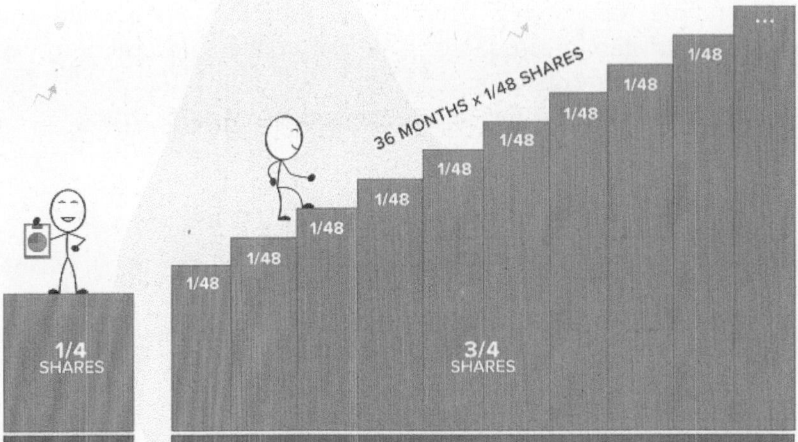

***Figure 3.5**: Founder vesting*

In share vesting the co-founder will not get any shares for the first 12 months. If everything works well in the first 12 months, then this co-founder will be given 25% shares and the rest of the shares can either vest months in 36 instalments over next 36 months or every year 25% shares can be vested.

This is a very important point to remember. If you vest shares to a co-founder immediately and things do not work out, then you are stuck with that co-founder for life even though that person may stop working in your startup.

Also, **salary** and **Employee Stock Options (ESOPs)** of a co-founder should be negotiated in advance and a written document should be created. There should be no ambiguity over these.

We have seen a lot of people failing financially due to disloyal and dishonest partners which means that you also need create safeguards relating to cheating in financial matters. During this, a few things need to be kept in mind, that the person who has authority and the approved signature, to sign in the bank can withdraw all the money at any time. Thus, this permission needs to be given with due precaution.

Moreover, no loans should be taken in a single partner's name as banks mainly pursue only those people in whose name the loan is taken. Similarly, only one partner should not give security for a bank loan as in case of default the bank will sell that security first for recovering money.

My principle for good partnership is that partners should share all assets and liabilities equally. This should be enforceable by legal contracts. Thus, do consult a good legal professional for creating these legal documents, while also taking the necessary precautions.

Core team

Once the startup starts building the product generally it becomes difficult for co-founders alone to run the startup. They need a small interdisciplinary team to help them. We term this initial small interdisciplinary team as the **core team**.

Figure 3.6: Core team

The Core team is very important for a startup. It does the initial work in a startup. During this time the strategy of the startup and features of the products change often. Thus, having a large team is not recommended as change becomes difficult with a large team.

Core team is a small team with people who are flexible and can-do multiple tasks. They are not too focused on external designations and want to act as internal entrepreneurs that is, **intrapreneurs**.

These people are not co-founders as they have not invested any money in the startup and generally take a salary along with **Employee Stock Options (ESOPs)**.

Finding such motivated and flexible people is a big challenge. Most employees work for external rewards in big organizations and thus you cannot just recruit anyone as a core team member. A core team member should be intrinsically motivated and willing to do something big as part of the startup. This person should not have a big ego. Ego at the initial stage in startups can be a big problem.

It is normal to interview 10 people and recruit just 1 person at this stage. Many big successful startups have done just that. Try to find people who have entrepreneurial skills but are willing to do a job due to financial reasons.

Sometimes you can also find such people from hackathons. You can even provide work initially to freelancers and then if the freelancer is particularly good in all aspects you can recruit the freelancer full time.

Some big successful entrepreneurs prefer to recruit failed entrepreneurs in the core team. They say that these people are entrepreneurs at heart who do jobs because of financial reasons.

Recruiting core team members is one of the most important things you do as a startup founder. Do not recruit the first 10 people for their low salary or great degree. Recruit them only if you feel they can contribute to your vision in an effective and flexible way.

How to remunerate early startup employees

A big issue in recruiting a good candidate in an early-stage startup is employee remuneration. Most early-stage startups cannot offer the same monthly salary to A-grade candidates which good corporates or big startups can give. An early-stage startup founder may feel that the competition for talent is not fair. Bigger organizations have an unfair advantage in recruiting talent. This is not the case. There are some sweeteners that only an early-stage startup can give.

This topic has been researched a lot and as a result a visual tool called **Remuneration Canvas** was created to communicate the options available to startups to remunerate high-quality talent.

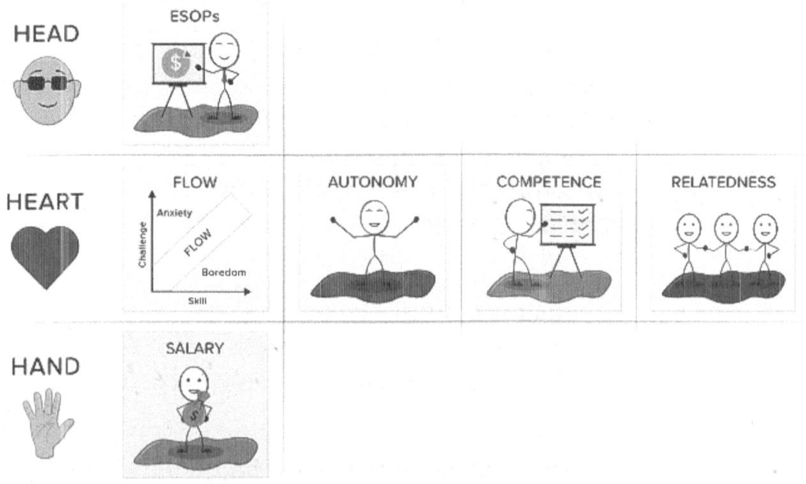

***Figure** 3.7: Remuneration canvas*

Now, we must look at employee compensation from 3 lenses:

- Head
- Hand
- Heart

In the lens of **'Head'**, we have named **Employee Stock Options (ESOPs)** since it motivates a potential employee to work in a startup logically. Any employee even if he or she works on a great salary will not become a multimillionaire if he or she does not get ESOPs. Also, the first few employees can get a bigger share of ESOPs than people following them. Hence let us say if someone gets 0.2% equity as an employee then if the startup becomes a USD 1 billion dollar valued the startup at a stage, then this employee's equity will be worth USD 2 million. Earning so much money in a regular corporate job is very difficult.

We will look at **Hand** second, since it concerns the in-hand salary. The in-hand salary will obviously be difficult to match for a startup when compared to established players in the industry. Here you can try to help the employee by customizing the package from the point of view of tax efficiency. Most big corporations do not structure the salary package for each employee whereas they have general salary structures which cannot be customized for every employee. The startup can take its small size as an advantage and offer each employee a tailor-made package that is more tax efficient.

Finally, we come to the lens of **'Heart'**. This is the biggest weapon in the arsenal of a startup when compared to a faceless big corporation. People work in big corporations for money. Corporates are heartless creatures who just become a machine to maximize shareholder wealth. The small early-stage startup is generally not funded and thus only shareholders are founders and other employees. A few family members of the founders may also be investors at this stage. Thus, the employee can be given psychological motivators by the founders. Usually, as observed psychological motivators have more power than any amount of salary or ESOPs.

Why do people leave Google or other big corporations for small startups?

The reasons are:

- **Flow:** Need for the right amount of challenge in work.

- **Self-determination theory:** Need for autonomy in the job, need for getting a feeling of competence and a feeling of relatedness.

Why do billionaires keep on working even though they can retire anytime they want? The reason is that humans crave challenges. People want just the right amount of challenge to stretch them at work. I read about the concept of **Flow** while designing and developing mobile games. The game designers know this psychological phenomenon and hook players by using this in game design.

Most corporate jobs are boring. Sometimes corporate and big startup jobs can make you anxious as they may challenge you more than you want. Startups due to their smaller size and better communication between the founders and employees can offer more fulfilling professional lives. An early-stage startup should try to design job roles to be having just the right amount of challenge for employees. If the challenge and skill set are just right the employee will be going into the **Flow** state often, where the employee will feel highly motivated and happy to work.

Another interesting and famous psychological theory I found while researching human motivation was **Self-Determination Theory**. It talks about providing **autonomy, competence,** and **relatedness** to a person to motivate him or her. Interestingly video games provide these also. Smaller startups can provide more autonomy to their employees. Also, every human feels good when it is communicated that they are competent. An early-stage startup founder can give direct feedback. Direct feedback is way more powerful than any corporate feedback process. Many corporations also do not have a proper feedback system.

A smaller startup, being small, encourages relatedness. In a 5,000-person company, you cannot get a proper feeling of relatedness in most positions. A smaller startup can feel like a family.

Thus, an early-stage startup should use psychological motivators to recruit and retain employees. These coupled with generous stock options and a decent salary allowing for day-to-day expenses will motivate employees who think long term and crave challenges.

Yes, there will be people who would not join startups for perks like free club memberships, gyms, food courts, the ability to buy flashy cars, etc., but those who will join, will join to contribute to growing the startup and having fun in that journey. They will be better employees in the long run for an early-stage startup.

Office versus remote work

Pre-Covid most people used to work in offices. Very few companies had policies for full remote work at that time. However, times have now changed. My own startup is now a fully online startup. As a startup you also need to take a decision on office versus remote work.

Figure 3.8: Office versus remote work

Office work provides some kinds of benefits while remote work provides some other kinds of benefits. Both the ways of working also have their own challenges. Some organizations like Paytm have shifted to hybrid work. This is a third option which many startups and corporations have chosen.

Office work as usual provides close high-quality interaction between people. Office work provides a lot of water cooler conversations which have their own benefits. Office work is offline and we human beings for ages have been doing offline work. Thus, office work has its own benefits.

Remote working is a new concept that has gained popularity after Covid, but it was being practiced by some startups and organizations ever since the internet came into the scene. Remote work became possible with the advent of the internet. Initially companies started remote offices in countries like India. Nowadays with the advent of services like Zoom, Google Drive, Basecamp etc., remote work has become very popular:

- Remote work provides lots of benefits to small early-stage startups. The first benefit is the saving of office expenses. 100% remote work means no office rent and no office maintenance. It also enables a more geographically spread-out team.

- Remote work allows small startups to recruit best talent at low cost in tier 2 and tier 3 cities. In my startup we have 2 people from very remote corners of India. Offline offices do not allow recruitment of such high-quality talent at affordable prices in metro cities.
- Remote work also provides more flexibility in working. Sometimes the distance does become a barrier but in a country like India which has the same time zone, remote work provides more opportunities than problems.
- Remote work is also good for work life balance. No daily commute and access to home cooked food greatly improves the quality of life of team members.

A big challenge in remote working is that holidays need to be provided based on the geographical location of the employee. For example, *Ganesh Chaturthi* is a holiday in Mumbai in India while it is a normal working day in the North of India. If the team is of an understanding nature, this challenge can easily be resolved.

Remote work does have its own challenges. Many people need constant policing and thus are not suited for remote work. Only people who can work on given targets independently are suited in companies doing remote work.

Moonlighting is another challenge which companies face. People start doing more than one job in remote jobs. This is a big issue in remote work.

Many companies have found that hybrid working gives some benefits of remote working while also giving some benefits of offline office working. Many companies these days, have 2- or 3-day offline offices. This allows high quality offline interactions and allows better work life balance.

As a startup choose what is best suited for you. Do consider remote working seriously as an option if you are an early-stage startup.

Human resources: Legal aspects

Human resources are essential for any startup to succeed. As a small early-stage startup, you need to also focus on legal aspects related to human resources. The most important thing you need to focus on is the **employment agreement**. Some lawyers also recommend a separate intellectual property agreement with employees.

Figure 3.9: Human Resources Legal Aspects

Hire a good lawyer and get a template created for employment agreement as per your needs. For those who do not have access to a lawyer, you can find such templates on the internet, although a good lawyer is always the best option for contract customization.

Employment agreement needs to mention salary, designation, intellectual property rights, etc. If doing work remotely work, you also need to be sensitive to certain other things like data being there on an employee's home computer. Thus, more data safety clauses may need to be inserted.

You also need to cut **Tax Deduction at Source (TDS)** on an employee's salary. Thus, it is also generally covered in employment agreement. The nature of work to be done by the employee is also covered in the employment agreement.

The company should also create templates for appointment letter, salary slip and relieving letter. These will be demanded by employees from time to time. The founders themselves will need to work these aspects as in a small early-stage startup there is no full-time human resource professional doing these tasks.

Some consultants and CAs / CPAs have started giving such HR services to startups. These services can also be made use of. Startup incubators also sometimes provide help in these legal aspects.

These legal aspects should be taken seriously from day one. In the long run whatever intellectual property you create needs to be defended from your employees too. Moreover, employees expect a professional company which has proper **Human Resource (HR)** policies and documentation.

Outsourcing versus internal development

A big question in product development is whether to create a product in house or outsource the product. A startup needs to do iterative development. This makes it difficult to outsource product development. In my experience vendors are generally not happy doing iterative development. They usually want to work with fixed specifications.

***Figure 3.10**: Vendor*

Thus, if you can find an employee to do work, in house, try to recruit that employee and get the work done in-house. A good way of outsourcing is to find freelancers who can be given projects on a piecemeal basis. Small projects can be outsourced to freelancers and iteration speed can be maintained without having an in-house full-time team.

If the vendor is willing to follow the agile project management approach, then you can outsource work to the vendor. Agile project management allows flexibility to change the features as per market needs. Outsourcing creates its own legal and human resource issues. The most important thing to do is to sign an outsourcing agreement with every vendor whether the vendor is a big company or a freelancer. The outsourcing agreement should clearly define the **Intellectual Property (IP)** rights and define the scope of the work, duration of work and its cost.

Also recruit a good IP lawyer who can give you advice on other documents required to be signed by vendors when applying for intellectual property rights. Some IP laws require specific documents to be signed by the creator of the intellectual property before assigning it to the final owner. Thus, getting timely advice on this is important.

Also, one must take care of the piracy aspect when outsourcing digital work. It is easier to stop piracy when you do the work in house. Do provide adequate legal protection for this in your outsourcing contract.

Furthermore, labor laws sometimes apply to outsourced teams. Prepare the contract in a way that labor laws do not apply to you as the outsourcer. Outsourcing contracts should be designed in a way that labor laws apply to vendors only.

My take on outsourcing versus internal development is that whatever you can do in house in the early stages of your startup, do it in house. Do not outsource for cost reasons unless the cost difference is too high. A startup needs high speed iterations which are many times not possible through outsourcing. Outsource only when it is a specialized task and you do not have talent inside the startup.

Do take care of legal aspects and piracy aspects while outsourcing as they are very important in the long run valuation of your startup.

Building a corporation

After reaching product market fit the scaling phase of the startup starts. In this phase you try to capture as much of the market as possible. This requires you to grow your manpower also very fast. At this stage the startup needs to morph from a core team-based structure to a departmentalized multi-team structure.

Figure 3.11: *Building a corporation*

A big technology startup generally has an elite team of **product managers** who define and manage the product development process. These are the superstars of the startup. A technology startup generally has a relatively big technology team which has various kinds of software developers. Lots of work is outsourced also from time to time with proper legal safeguards.

***Figure 3.12:** Key departments in a tech startup*

The largest number of people in any fast-growing startups are usually in sales and marketing. These combined are generally called the business team. People in the business team are usually many times the people in the technology team which itself is many times the number of people in the product management team.

Finally, there are support teams in the form of administration, audit, human resources, recruitment, finance and purchase etc. These teams are important for the smooth functioning of the organization. Although these teams do not directly create the product their role is no less important than the product teams.

Any big corporation needs people with multiple seniority levels. Generally, in a big organization there are 4 types of seniority levels. At the top are **Chief Executive Officer (CEO), Chief Operating Officer (COO)** and **President**, etc.

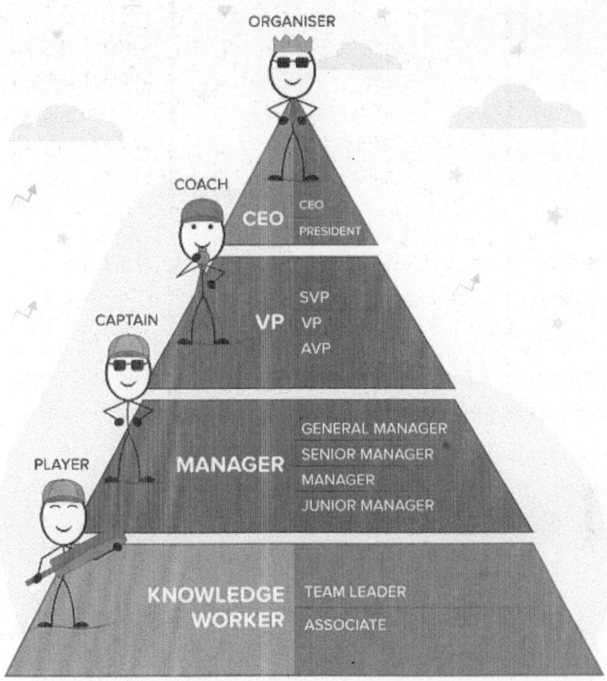

Figure 3.13: *Seniority Levels*

At the second level there are **Vice Presidents (VPs)**. Bigger companies can have **Senior Vice Presidents (SVP)** and **Assistant Vice Presidents (AVP).** Smaller companies have just a few VPs. Large unicorn startups can have many VPs. The VP generally has full control over a department or a big team.

At the third level are the **managers**. The managers can be of multiple types. You can have designations like **junior manager**, **manager**, **senior manager**, and **general manager**. These are the people who lead the actual execution of day-to-day tasks.

At the fourth level we have **knowledge workers**. These are the actual people who do executional tasks in a startup. Obviously, most people in the company are at this level.

This is the broad overview you should be knowing while building a corporation.

Conclusion

All the work in a startup must be done by humans whether directly or indirectly. For running a high growth startup, understanding human behavior, and managing human resources is a must. Successful startup founders are experts in managing human resources. Hence, we focused on understanding the aspects related to co-founders, core team and scaling the organization.

In the next chapter, we will focus on getting money for our startup. We will cover the various types of investors and their expectations from us. We will also learn about the art of making a good pitch deck and legal aspects related to funding.

CHAPTER 4
Purchasing Power

Introduction

Every startup needs money to grow. The process of raising this money is called **funding**.

Initially, every startup must bootstrap that is, founders must invest their own money in the startup. At start some friends or family members may be willing to invest money in a startup. These days a startup may also get some financial assistance from various incubators and government schemes.

Once the startup has clarity on the product and has created a **Minimum Viable Product (MVP)** the startup can raise money from professional angel investors. After product market fit the startup's ability to raise money increases a lot and usually raising millions of dollars from venture capitalists becomes possible.

In this series of topics, I am sharing all these aspects with you. Plus, we will be exploring ways of increasing your startup's purchasing power. Purchasing power refers to the process of raising money for the startup as well as ways in which you can get purchasing power even without raising any money.

Figure 4.1: *Purchasing power*

Structure

This chapter will cover the following topics:

- What is bootstrapping?
- Startup CFO
- Introduction to incubators and accelerators
- Introduction to angel investors
- Introduction to Venture Capitalists
- How to contact investors?
- Managing a cap table
- How to create a great pitch desk?
- What is a term sheet?
- Should I take funding?
- What if I fail?

Objectives

This chapter is designed to be a comprehensive guide for entrepreneurs navigating the intricate landscape of startup funding. It begins with a foundational exploration of bootstrapping, elucidating the concept of self-funding as a viable option. The role of a Startup CFO is then introduced, shedding light on financial strategies crucial for success. The chapter delves into the ecosystem of incubators, accelerators, angel investors, and venture capitalists, providing insights into their functions and how to approach them. Practical guidance on contacting investors and managing a cap table is covered, followed by essential insights on crafting an impactful pitch deck. The discussion extends to understanding term sheets, contemplating the decision to seek funding, and addressing the potential challenges of failure. By the end of this chapter, readers will be equipped with the knowledge needed to navigate funding options and make informed decisions vital for the growth and sustainability of their startup ventures.

What is bootstrapping?

Bootstrapping is a term used to describe the fact that the startup is being funded by the founders themselves and no outside investment has been taken. Initially, only the founders believe in a startup's potential. Thus, only they fund the startup. Very rarely do external investors invest in a startup at the initial stage.

External funding in the initial stages generally happens when the founders have high credentials. External investors generally invest only after the problem solution fit has been established. External investors want clarity of the problem, the solution proposed and some idea of the potential to scale before investing:

***Figure 4.2:** Bootstrapping*

Thus, in the initial period bootstrapping is more of a compulsion than an option. It has both advantages and disadvantages. The advantages are the following:

- Bootstrapping allows founders to experiment on their own terms without any poking from investors.
- Bootstrapping allows founders to retain ownership in the startup. The later founders raise money the better it is in terms of their long-term shareholding.
- Bootstrapping also allows founders to postpone incorporation as a company longer. Investors generally want company incorporation before investing. Generally, that involves cost and paperwork which should be avoided till there is clarity on the problem and proposed solution.
- Bootstrapping also allows the startup to be in stealth mode for longer.

The following are the disadvantages of bootstrapping:

- Many potential employees look forward to validation from reputed external investors before joining a startup. Generally, employees from corporations do not want to join a bootstrapped startup.
- Many vendors do not want to work with bootstrapped startups thinking that the startup can close anytime. They prefer startups that have been funded by reputed investors.
- External funding provides a valuation to the company for pricing its equity. This is helpful for using ESOPs as a recruitment tool.

I personally feel that startups should not raise money till they have some clarity on the problem they're trying to solve, the solution being created and somewhat of an idea of the scaling potential. This allows for getting better valuations from investors and saves entrepreneurs from feeling frustrated due to investor rejections. Frustration due to investor rejections is a big cause of startup closure. Many investors will still reject funding a startup after the problem solution fit however the probability of the funding will be more and the founders would be more confident in their startup's potential.

Another question related to the bootstrapping stage is at what time should one or more founders join a startup full time? According to me the founders should join a startup full time when they feel a need to do so, and they can afford it (refer to *Figure 4.3*):

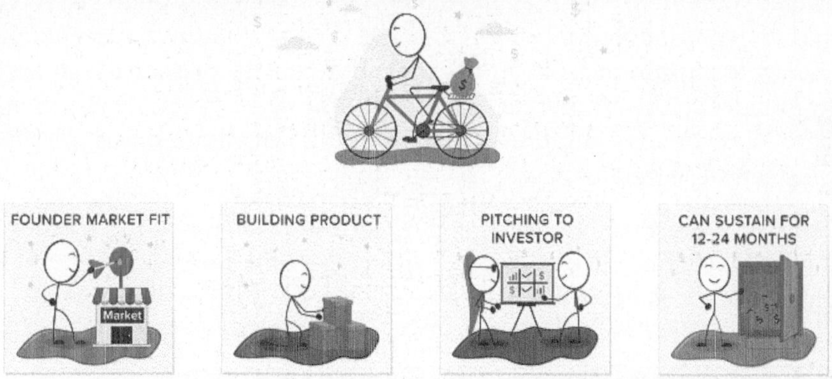

***Figure 4.3**: When should you join your startup full time?*

Founders should, however, start the bootstrapping phase part-time. After some time when they get clarity on the problem and a solution to prototype, they may explore joining the startup full time.

However, before joining, full-time founders should explore the following points:

- The founders should start loving the problem and feel that the solution is executable. It is preferable if one or more founders feel at ease in the domain of the problem due to their prior experience.
- The founders should analyze it if their involvement is required full time to develop the product.
- If the startup has achieved problem solution fit or is close to achieving it, then it can start pitching to investors. Investors generally want the founders to be working full time in the startup and thus at that time the founders should shift full time to the startup.
- The most important decision point should be the availability of money to sustain the startup and the families of the founders. Generally, the startup founders should have at least 12 months of money to run the startup since it may take time to create a minimum viable product and raise funding from angel investors. If the startup has money for 24 months, it is generally better as product development sometimes takes longer in the case of some products.

Hence, founders should consider joining the startup full-time only when they believe it is necessary for creating a fully developed product and are confident that they have identified the right problem to solve and explored potential solutions. Also, they should have enough money to sustain the startup full time. If money is an issue the startup founders should continue to work part-time or at least try to do some parallel revenue generation activity (but not very time consuming) till they can raise the funding.

Thus, we see that bootstrapping is an essential part of a startup's journey and should be planned properly to avoid the fate of premature closure of the startup.

Startup CFO

Startups are about building and selling products, recruiting and managing people, and raising funding. Unfortunately, we live in a world where laws are complex and impact all these activities. Additionally, a startup is also a company and thus laws related to the formation and management of companies also apply to it.

A big company generally has a **Chief Financial Officer (CFO)** who manages all legal and financial aspects of the company. In a small startup, this role must be done by one or more founders. Thus, as a startup founder, you need to learn a little bit of law and accounts as well so that your business can grow and be in safe hands (refer to *Figure 4.4*):

***Figure 4.4**: Startup CFO*

Laws in any country are multiple and complex. You do not need to learn everything for running a startup but you just need to focus on a few aspects like corporate laws, tax laws, contract laws, Intellectual Property (IP) laws and employment laws.

Company formation

To form a company, you need to incorporate it under the **corporate laws** of your country. Corporate laws are generally complex and allow you to form a company with the following:

- **Share capital:** The capital with which the company will work.
- **Shareholders:** The people who have put in capital and own the company.
- **Directors:** The people who will run the company.
- **Registered office:** The registered physical place of business of the company.

Generally, it is advisable to form a company with the help of a professional who specializes in company laws. In India, generally such a professional is a **Chartered Accountant (CA)** or **Company Secretary (CS)**. The government has tried to make everything digital and fast but unfortunately, government fails to understand product management and thus digital processes are pathetic at times.

An important example is that digital signatures in India do not work on any Apple computer! Thus, I really miss the old system of the paper-based company formation process since complying with digital processes can be a pain. I had to courier my digital signature token to the CA physically to make her sign the incorporation documents on my behalf!

The second focus area pertains to tax laws, which can be categorized into two types: direct and indirect. Direct tax laws, such as income tax, apply directly to the taxpayer on their income. In contrast, indirect tax laws, exemplified by **Goods and Services Tax (GST),** apply indirectly through the product provider. Individuals pay income tax on their earnings, while GST is paid to the provider of goods or services. The provider, mandated by the government, collects and remits the GST to the government for the provided goods or services.

Income tax

Income tax is complicated but after being a **Chartered Accountant (CA)** myself I would like to tell you that Income Tax is one of the most well-formulated laws in India. It is relatively straightforward once you start understanding it. Broadly you need to learn about a few major concepts so that you can talk to your CA in a little technical jargon and get the income tax returns (tax documents) filed in a timely manner.

The first concept of Income Tax in India is the **Permanent Account Number (PAN)**. When you register the company, you get a PAN automatically. PAN is easy to apply online also. PAN is the number through which the income tax department and government tracks all transactions. For techies, it is your primary key value in the government's database.

Income tax allows multiple types of taxpayers. Some of the most prominent types allowed are individual, partnership firm and company. A startup will mostly be incorporated as a **private limited company** although **Limited Liability Partnership (LLP)** is also a practical option in the initial phase. The entrepreneur will have to file a separate income tax return of the company.

The **income tax return** is a tax report you need to file yearly, with the income tax department. Unfortunately, our finance ministers have been legal professionals instead of being product managers or UX designers. Thus, the tax return software provided by the government is often buggy and very complex. Even as a CA I hate spending hours filing my own return. It took 4-5 hours last time for me to fill in all the details in my own personal income tax return. Even though I am a CA, and to save time I have outsourced filing of my startup's return to another CA! Thus, please do not file your own returns. Focus on creating and selling a good product instead of wasting time yourself filing income tax returns. Try to find a good income tax professional who is a CA or a lawyer who can file your tax returns.

Income tax law categorizes income into 5 types:

- Income from salary
- Income from house property (rent)
- Income from business or profession
- Income from capital gains
- Income from other sources (interest, dividend, etc.)

A startup will generally have income from business or profession. Many companies used to make black money white by taking capital from bogus sources at a premium. Thus, income tax law has stringent provisions regarding taking of capital by issuing shares at a premium.

Unfortunately, this law creates a lot of problems for startups that generally get funding at a high premium. This problem is popularly known as **angel tax**. Fortunately, the government allows startups that are registered under Startup India some exemptions from angel tax. It is one of the easiest procedures ever laid down by the government and is completely free of any red tape or corruption. You can very easily go to the Startup India website and apply and if needed CAs also help in getting this registration.

Finally, you need to also understand the concept of **Tax Deduction at Source (TDS)**. Many taxpayers are obliged by law to collect the tax of the receiving party and deposit such tax monthly. Some of the transactions on which TDS is applicable in payment of salaries to employees whose incomes are either taxable, or are payments above a threshold to professionals or contractors, etc. Payment on rent above a limit also needs tax deduction while paying rent. This is a very important tax law and thus a startup founder should consult a tax professional for the current thresholds and rates. The biggest grievance I have against the income tax department is that they change tax rates and thresholds too often. Thus, it becomes nearly impossible for the common man to do anything without consulting a practicing tax professional. A big pain for entrepreneurs running small startups is the monthly deposit of TDS and the filing of quarterly TDS returns.

Goods and Services Tax (GST)

Goods and Services Tax (GST) is also a complex law. You generally need to apply to the government for collecting GST in India if you earn a revenue above a certain threshold. You will get a GST number when you register. Generally, for GST you need to file multiple monthly GST returns. For small taxpayers the government allows the option to file returns quarterly also. Generally, the GST law is very complex so I will advise you to hire a good CA for this. A big pain for tech entrepreneurs like me is that GST returns for a company cannot be filed without a government-recognized digital signature. Unfortunately, none of them work on an Apple computer and many do not work on some Windows PCs also. Thus, you may need to physically send the digital signature dongle to your tax professional!

Contract law

Next, you need to understand the **contract law**. Contracts are the lifeblood of any business. As per my knowledge you can also make contracts orally without any documentation. The only issue is that in case of a dispute you will not have any proof of the contract. Thus, it is advisable to make written contracts. For small things, I personally prefer written emails however, for bigger or important contracts generally, it is advisable to engage a lawyer to create a contract and attach a stamp paper of appropriate value to the contract documentation. You can also get templates of contracts like a rent agreement, a Non-Disclosure Agreement (NDA), etc., online.

Intellectual property laws

Intellectual Property (IP) laws are also very important for a startup. Copyright gives you protection from someone using your content, code, or design without your consent. Patent refers to monopoly you get over your inventions. Trademark refers to protection you get over your trade names.

You need to understand that you automatically get a **copyright** on every piece of content, code, or design you make. For content, code, or design that your employees create you need to have explicit IP assignment to the company in the employment contracts. For work, you get done from contractors or freelancers, you need to have a contract in place which has an explicit clause for IP assignment. Generally, it is advisable to get an employment contract or contractor contract template from a good lawyer so that there are no legal issues later. Copyrights need not be applied explicitly but for important content like films, books, game characters, etc., it is advisable to apply for copyright explicitly.

Any invention you make can be patented and you can get a monopoly on that for many years. **Patents** are expensive and difficult to get. Also, in the age of lean startup, many times patents are not useful as the startup may pivot before even getting a patent!

Trademarks should generally be registered for your trade name. You may also register a trademark for an app name or website name. The government gives a rebate on registration fees if you are registered under **Startup India program** or as a **Medium, Small or Micro Enterprise (MSME)**. For registration of trademark, copyright, and patents you should contact a good IP lawyer.

Law related to employees

Finally, you need to have an **employment contract** with employees and have proper IP protection built in the agreement. For part-time employees or freelancers also, have some sort of legal agreement in place. Beyond a certain number of employees, you need to register under labor laws also. Generally, for a startup with less than 10 employees, you do not need any such registration although these days during company formation in India every company is registered under labor laws.

Accounts and audit

You also need to have someone who can make your **accounts** as per the double-entry system of accounts. You need to file yearly final accounts like a balance sheet, profit and loss account and cash flow statement with the **Ministry of Company Affairs (MCA)** and **Income Tax department**.

You also need an **auditor**. In India, only a practicing-chartered accountant can be an auditor. Every year an auditor must audit your accounts and give you an audit report. This report must be filed with the MCA. Above a certain threshold of revenue, even the income tax department wants a separate tax audit report for which you will need to hire a CA. Many times, the same auditor does both audits.

Thus, you see it is not easy to be an entrepreneur. You need to become a semi-legal professional to run your startup. I sometimes find these things complicated even though I am a CA, thus I will recommend you get one or more legal professionals who can help you through this.

Introduction to incubators and accelerators

Once upon a time the entrepreneur was alone in his or her path to startup success. There was no support from the startup ecosystem. This made surviving tough. Getting mentorship and funding was very difficult.

This has changed now. These days lots of startup incubators and accelerators have sprung up (refer to *Figure 4.5*). Governments around the world are also promoting startup incubators. For example, in India there are lots of government startup programs which are supporting funding to startup incubators. Many educational institutions also have startup incubators these days. The startup incubators at the prestigious **Indian Institute of Technology (IITs)** are very active and the good thing is that they allow incubation facilities to non-IITian entrepreneurs too:

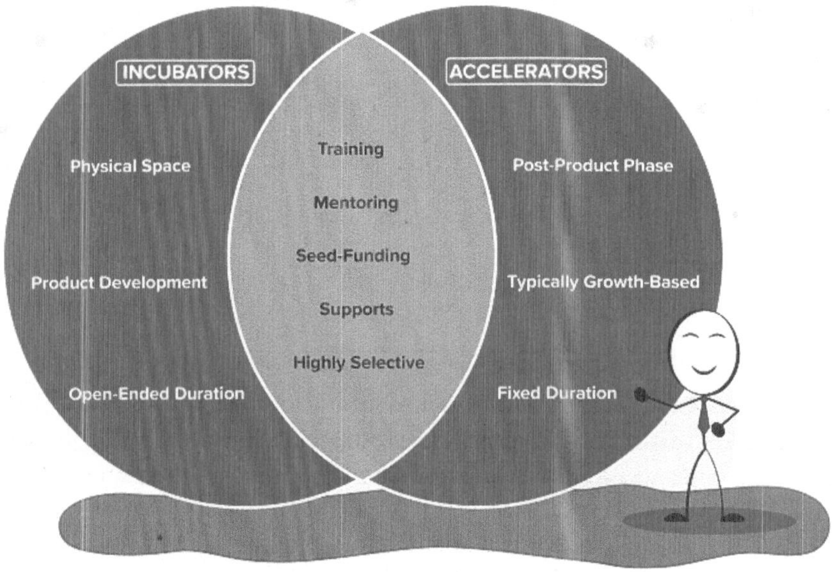

Figure 4.5*: Incubators and accelerators*

Generally, startup incubators are very helpful to early-stage startups. They provide mentoring, infrastructure, and funding to newborn companies. The startup incubators too, have an eligibility criteria for the selection of startups. This eligibility criteria in turn, is determined by the government scheme which funds startup incubators.

Most startup incubators prior to Covid wanted startups to operate out of their premises. After Covid, many startup incubators allowed virtual incubation also. Startup incubators have tie-ups with various important organizations like Amazon, Google and Microsoft and provide free credits for AWS, Google Cloud, Azure also to their incubates.

If you are a first-time startup founder, then I would recommend you join a startup incubator as that will help you in multiple ways. Startup incubators connect startups to investors also.

Startup Accelerators have become very popular over the last decade. The reason has been the super success of the Y Combinator startup accelerator program in the US. Startup accelerators generally take startups in groups (also called cohorts) and try to accelerate them over a period of 3 to 6 months. Through intense mentoring, networking, and a little bit of funding these programs push a startup to achieve growth at a fast pace. These startup accelerators also showcase startups to big investors at the end of the program and thus they provide an excellent opportunity for startups to grow.

Introduction to angel investors

Startups need funding. Initially, founders fund a startup. After that at times, friends and family members also contribute to the startup's capital. These friends and family members act as angels to the startup and invest their money generally on just the relationship with the founder(s). After these sources are exhausted generally a startup must look outside for funding and the first people a startup can approach for funding are professional **Angel Investors.**

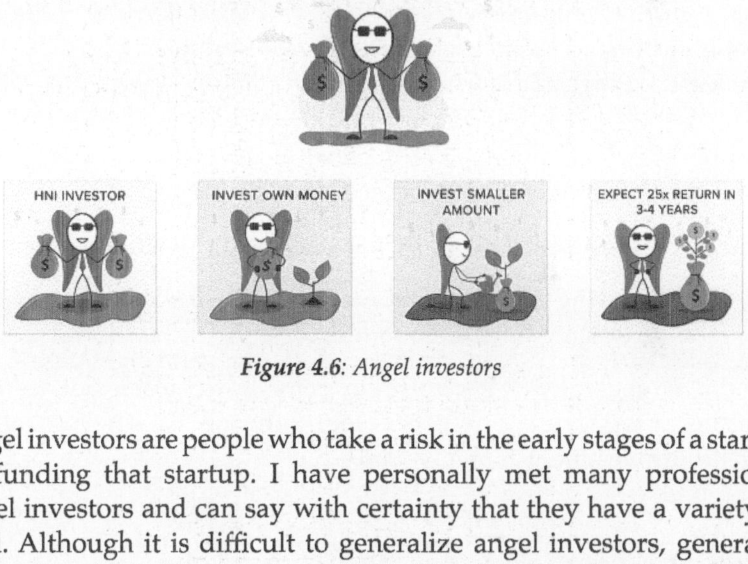

***Figure 4.6**: Angel investors*

Angel investors are people who take a risk in the early stages of a startup by funding that startup. I have personally met many professional angel investors and can say with certainty that they have a variety as well. Although it is difficult to generalize angel investors, generally, professional angel investors are **High Net Worth Individuals (HNIs)** who want to invest their own money in the early stages of a startup. They want large returns. Some want 10x returns while others want 100x returns. However, we can safely say that most angel investors want 10x to 25x return in 2 to 4 years.

Angel investors generally invest smaller sums of money than full-fledged venture capitalists. In India generally, angel investors invest anywhere between Rs 5 lakh (USD 6,000) to Rs 1 crore (USD 120,000).

Angel investors sometimes also form networks. These are called **angel networks**. Angel networks allow individual angel investors to get economies of scale in certain areas like due diligence and the ability to access large pockets of startups. For example, many angel networks reach out to renowned universities in the USA and IITs in India for investment. It will be difficult for an individual angel investor to reach out to startups in these institutions at a large scale.

Another big benefit of angel networks is that they allow angel investors to pool in money and invest together. That reduces significant risk for angel investors. I know of big angel networks in India that allow many investors to invest as low as Rs. 500,000 in multiple startups. This hedging reduces risk considerably for the individual investor.

Angel networks also have standard legal processes and thus individual investors find it convenient to invest through them.

Thus, a budding entrepreneur should try to reach out to both individual angel investors and angel networks. Angel investors generally focus on at least 4 things in a startup before investing:

- Personal qualities of the **founder(s)**
- The **problem** which is being solved by the startup
- The **solution** finalized by the startup to solve the problem
- The **scaling** potential and probability of the potential solution to be executed by the founders

Thus, it is generally better for entrepreneurs to reach out to angel investors after arriving at a **problem solution fit**. The probability of getting investment is many times higher after achieving problem solution fit.

The entrepreneur should create an **elevator pitch**. Elevator pitch is a 2–3-line introduction to the startup. Within 30 seconds to 1 minute, the entrepreneur should be able to introduce the startup to the potential investor. If within that time the investor does not hook up, then generally the investor will not go ahead and ask for a **pitch deck**.

A **pitch deck** is a slide deck that lists out the following information as clearly as possible:

- Elevator pitch
- Problem

- Solution
- Why now?
- Market
- Product
- Why us?
- Business Model
- Team
- Financials

If the angel investor likes the pitch deck, he or she will generally want to explore the startup more. A few rounds of discussions will be held with the founders and sometimes even the core team. The angel investor will also do some initial due diligence and if all goes well then, the professional angel investor will sign a **'term sheet'** with the startup. After the term sheet signing the angel investor will generally do detailed **due diligence**. Due diligence is the checking of various legal documents, financial statements, and physical verification by the representatives of the investor.

Once due diligence is complete and no big issues are found, the investor will sign definitive legal documents for the investment and give the money according to the agreed schedule and milestones.

Individual investors may focus less on some legal aspects due to logistical issues but generally, angel networks do follow the proper due diligence and the process described above.

The biggest question an early-stage startup founder has during the initial period is how to reach out to potential angel investors. In my experience, there are multiple ways of reaching out to professional angel investors. A good way is to attend big startup conferences. Conferences like SXSW in Austin, USA or conferences organized by The Indus Entrepreneurs (TiE) in India and the USA are good events for this.

Another way to reach out to angel investors is to reach out to them on Twitter or LinkedIn. All investors may not reply to the messages but if you write to 10 investors, some of them will reply.

A good way, which most investors prefer is to reach out through some person in the network of the investor. Try to build a strong network with people in the startup ecosystem. They can refer you to their angel investor friends. Becoming part of the incubation programs at startup incubators and startup accelerator programs do help here. Incubators and startup accelerator programs have good connections with investors. Their reference carries weight in the industry.

Another tried and tested way to success, is to create some social media buzz around your startup. That really helps to reach out to investors. Investors are more receptive to cold emails and messages from startups they have heard about.

Another good way is to reach out to angel networks. Angel networks have professional processes for vetting startups. You can reach out to them through their websites. For example, this is the link to such a page on the website of Indian Angel Network (one of the most reputed angel networks in India): **https://www.indianangelnetwork.com/dashboard/submit-new-plan**.

Another good way to get to angel investors these days is to take part in professional pitching contests. Many organizations like government startup programs and TiE etc., hold such pitching contests. They generally call professional angel investors and senior executives from big startups for judging these contests. If these people like your pitch they will be receptive. These people may become potential investors or introducers to investors.

The most important thing at this stage is the network. The bigger and deeper your network, the better it is. If you are in India or USA, I would recommend joining the local chapter of **The Indus Entrepreneurs (TiE).** They do a lot of events and initiatives to help entrepreneurs increase their network and reach out to professional investors.

Getting angel funding is important for many startups who do not have enough capital to sail through the 'build' stage. If you have multiple co-founders, then one co-founder should spend a large amount of his or her time on building the network with investors and pitching in front of them.

Finally, I would like to tell you that not every angel investor will fund you. Some of the most iconic startups we admire today had to go to multiple investors before getting any funding. Thus, if you must reach out to 10 potential investors for getting funding from just 1 investor do not lose heart. This is normal in the funding process. I have seen entrepreneurs closing startups after talking to 3-4 investors. Do not lose confidence. Almost every investor will ask tough questions. Try to learn from the experience and prepare your answers to these questions, as your journey continues.

Angel investors can provide more value than just money. They can give you free mentoring and a built-in network. Do not choose angel investors only for money. Focus on knowledge, experience and network they will bring along with money. Try to deduce all these parameters before taking funding from an angel investor. Another important thing that angel investors can bring is their reputation. If an iconic angel investor invests in your startups, you will get media coverage, better employees, better funding later, etc.

Thus, angel investors are an important ingredient in the success of a startup. Choose them wisely and with proper preparation. A good angel investor will become a steppingstone in your startup's growth and may also introduce you at later stages to potential venture capitalists.

Introduction to Venture Capitalists

Venture Capitalists (VCs) are professionals who manage funds that invest money into startups. Unlike angel investors, venture capitalists are generally more process oriented and invest larger sums of money.

Venture capital firms launch venture capital funds from time to time. Venture capital funds raise capital from investors like high-net-worth individuals, family offices of wealthy individuals, endowments, foundations, pension funds, etc. Venture capital funds generally operate for a period of 8 to 12 years. Venture capital funds are generally regulated by the government.

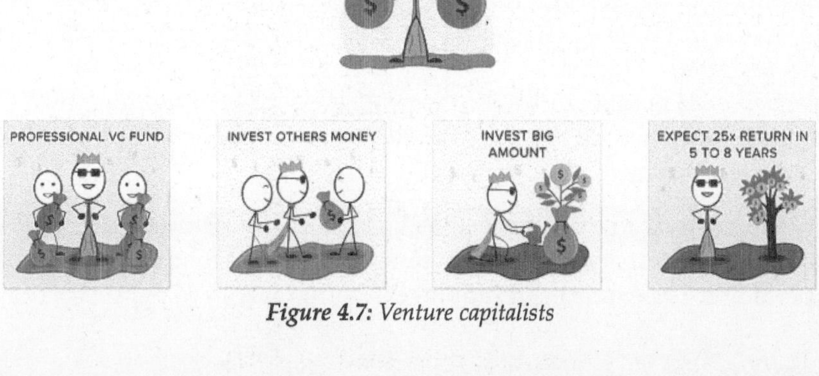

Figure 4.7: Venture capitalists

Venture capital funds have 2 kinds of investors. The people who start and operate the fund are called **'General Partners' (GP)**. GPs invest some money of their own when they start a venture capital fund. The investors who do not manage the fund and only supply capital are called **'Limited Partners' (LP)**.

There are hundreds of venture capital firms worldwide. Countries like the USA, China and India have many of them. Many VCs are present in multiple countries. Some of the world-famous venture capital firms are:

- Sequoia Capital
- Kleiner Perkins Caufield and Byers
- Andreesen Horowitz
- Accel

The focus of every venture capitalist is to find the startups which can give a large return. A good startup will return 25x or more in 5 to 8 years. The reason VCs focus on high returns is that VCs generally lose money on 5 out of 10 startups they invest in. In 2-3 out of 10 they generally get the capital back or maximum double the capital invested. In only 1-2 startups out of 10, the good VCs get a large return. The venture capitalists focus on getting a few investments right out of the whole portfolio. This is very different from the traditional investment approach taken by other kinds of investors.

A question that generally comes to mind is when a startup should raise money from a venture capitalist. The answer is based on the lifecycle of the startup, the profitability of the startup and the willingness of the founders to part with some control of the startup to investors.

VCs generally want to invest only if the startup has achieved product market fit. At product market fit the startup has a high demand for the product and there is high customer retention. VCs however sometimes do invest in other cases also based on the market, product potential and pedigree of founders. Thus, if the product market fit has not been reached or is nowhere in sight the probability of being funded by VCs is quite low. I would advise founders to focus on achieving product market fit before going to meet VCs.

The other thing to consider is that VCs generally require a seat on the board of directors and put restrictions on certain aspects of a startup's operations. For example, it is quite common for VCs to put restrictions related to the appointment of auditors, raising of future capital, or selling founder's equity without their approval, etc.

Thus, if the business can generate near term cash flows many experts advise the startups to focus on getting funds from banks. In case the profitability will take a long run to achieve and cash flows would be low in the initial period and very high in the long run then VC funding is the only good option for getting large pools of capital.

Most major technology companies have been funded by venture capitalists in the initial days. For example, Apple, Google, Amazon, Facebook, etc. were also funded by VCs in the initial days. Thus, venture capitalists may be a relatively small group of investors worldwide, but venture capitalists have changed the face of the planet.

Suggested reading:

- 'Secrets of Sand Hill Road' by *Scott Kupor*
- Mastering the VC Game: A Venture Capital Insider Reveals How to Get from Start-up to IPO on Your Terms

How to contact investors

Every startup that intends to take external funding must reach out to external investors at some point. You can reach investors at 2 stages. The first stage where you can reach investors is after finding the problem solution fit. At this stage you should reach out to angel investors.

Angel investors can be reached out in various ways. The best way of reaching out to an investor is through a common contact. If you know someone who knows the angel investor and he or she recommends you to the angel investor, the angel investor will take you more seriously.

Figure 4.8: *Contacting Investors*

Another way of reaching investors is to join some startup ecosystem organizations in your area. A good example of such an organization in the USA and India is **The Indus Entrepreneurs (TiE).** In India, **Alliance of Digital India Foundation (ADIF)** is also a good organization to join. I am connected to both the organizations on a personal level.

If you can make a name for yourself on social media and somehow reach the feed of your target investors, you will find it easier to reach your goal. Investors love to track various entrepreneurs and startups and being popular on social media and that is one way of increasing your reach within the investor community.

Cold calling or cold emails are generally not very effective but can be tried if there are no other options available. Moreover, many angel investors are organized as angel investment networks and have a website where you can reach out to them.

You can also get connected to angel investors and venture capitalists through startup incubators and startup accelerators. Thus, joining an incubator or accelerator is a good strategy for getting connected to investors.

Venture capitalists can also be reached out in a similar way, but they generally want the startup to have achieved the product market fit before investing. If the founder is an iconic founder, then this rule sometimes does not apply!

Venture capitalists are generally well organized and have junior team members scouting for good startups and entrepreneurs. If you can get some press coverage, then you can get these people to contact you also. When I left Paytm, my startup got press coverage and lots of big investors reached out to me for investment. The only problem was that I had just started my startup 1 week ago and thus was not very investable!

Managing cap table

Cap table is a very important term. Cap table refers to the capital table or the ownership structure of a startup. Initially the entrepreneurs own 100% capital of the startup. Sometimes they give shares to their family members from the point of view of tax planning or to comply with company incorporation laws.

Specific types of companies need a specified minimum number of shareholders. For example, in India a normal private limited company needs a minimum 2 shareholders. A public limited company needs at least 7 shareholders. Indian laws also allow one person company.

The startup needs to provide **Employee Stock Options (ESOPs)** to motivate the employees. Thus, generally most startups keep 5% to 10% of equity for ESOPs. Generally, ESOPs need to be negotiated keeping in mind the seniority and importance of people in the core team. Moreover, the ESOPs need to be given in a 4 or 5-year vesting period. It basically means that if you give someone 1,000 shares in your startup, give them 250 shares per year in a span of 4 years instead of out rightly give them 1,000 shares. The basic aim of providing ESOPs is to retain the employees for the long run.

Startups at times need to provide equity to mentors. Vesting 2 to 4 years is a useful concept. Mentors can take anywhere from 0.5% to 2-3% of equity according to their profile and the time being provided.

Then come the investors. Generally, one should not dilute more than 20% equity in any funding round. There are multiple funding rounds. The first round is generally the friends and family round. It is generally followed by funding from professional angel investors. Then comes the series A funding round where venture capitalists come into the picture properly. Series A is followed by series B, series C and so on.

How to create a great pitch deck

Most startups need funding from external investors. External investors need to be introduced to a startup's growth potential to make them ready to invest money. The pitch deck is a brief presentation that allows investors and other stakeholders to get an idea about the business of the startup.

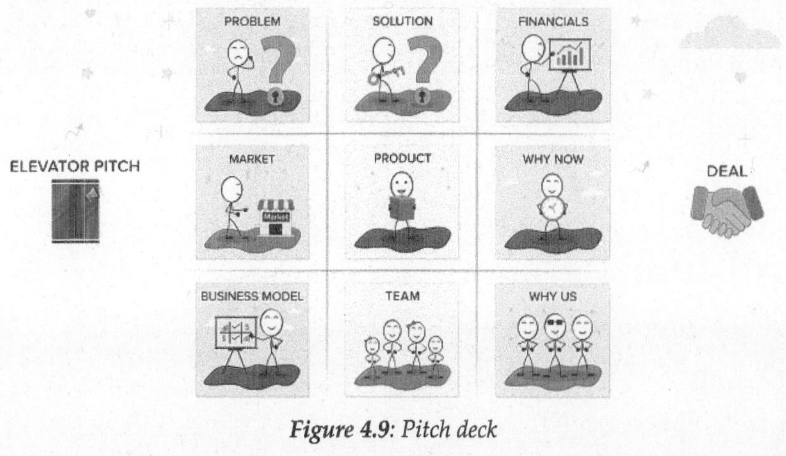

***Figure 4.9**: Pitch deck*

Pitch deck should tell the story of your startup. Storytelling skills are very important while pitching. The investors need to be convinced that your startup is a good future story to invest in.

The pitch deck should generally be as concise as possible while also giving relevant details. According to my experience, the following information should be included in a pitch deck:

- Introductory Slide (elevator pitch)
- Problem
- Solution
- Why now?
- Market
- Product
- Why us?
- Business model
- Team
- Financials
- Deal

Elevator pitch

The entrepreneur should create an **elevator pitch**. Elevator pitch is a 2–3-line introduction to the startup. Within 30 seconds to 1 minute, the entrepreneur should be able to introduce the startup to the potential investor. This first slide acts as an interesting hook for the rest of the presentation. If you cannot hook the investor with the elevator pitch, then the investor may not listen to the whole presentation attentively.

For example, the elevator pitch of my startup, Fun2Do Labs is very simple: *We are making a Doraemon-like story world through which we can teach primary school kids.*

Problem

Startups exist to solve problems and provide a solution. The problem should be big enough and urgent enough to interest the investor.

Solution

A startup should be able to devise a good solution to the problem described above. The solution should be desirable, viable and feasible. A startup should talk about the solution and its major points in the pitch deck.

Why now?

Investors generally ask about the right timing. They generally ask why someone has not created a good solution to this big problem to date. The startup should have a good answer to this question.

Market

The startup needs to define the potential market, its size and the structure. The startup needs to share the following 3 things related to market size:

Total Addressable Market (TAM)

The total market size if the company can reach everyone who can use the solution.

For example, a company building a Netflix kind of video streaming solution can say that there are 4 billion people having access to the internet. If everyone pays USD 5 a month then the total addressable market is USD 5 x 12 x 4 billion = USD 240 billion.

Serviceable Available Market (SAM)

Serviceable Available Market (SAM) is the portion of TAM targeted and served by a company's products or services.

In our above example, this will be people who have access to high-speed internet as Netflix type of solution cannot be used without high-speed internet. Also, people may need to have either a TV or a mobile phone. It will also be useful only to those people who can be covered with the available content. So, say if we have content in a few languages that will further restrict the number of potential users. Thus, say only 1 billion people can be covered with the above restrictions. So, the serviceable available market (SAM) will be USD 5 x 12 x 1 billion = USD 60 billion.

Serviceable Obtainable Market (SOM)

Serviceable Obtainable Market (SOM) refers to the share of the market which the company can get through its products. In the above example assume we have 5 big competitors including Netflix and Disney. Thus, the company may estimate getting a 20% market share in the long term. Then the serviceable obtainable market (SOM) will be 20% of SAM i.e. USD 12 billion.

Product

The startup needs to show the product. If a demo is ready, it should be shown. If showing a demo is not practical, then preferably a video of it can be included. At least a slide showing the product visually along with the main features should be there.

Why us?

This is a very important slide. The startup founders need to tell why they and their team will be able to beat the competition.

Business model

The startup needs to define the business model. In case it is an internet based business the business model may be one of the few prominent ones:

- Paid App
- Freemium App
- Ad support content
- Software as a service (SaaS)
- Content Subscription
- E-Commerce
- Uber for X (Uber kind of physical service delivery using the Internet and apps)

The potential revenue, fixed and variable cost curves can also be shown to give a better idea of the power of the business model.

Team

The startup needs to share details of the founders and the major members of the team. The educational qualifications and experience of the founders and major team members are generally shared. The details of mentors may also be shared here.

Financials

The financials should also be shared if the startup has been operating for more than a few months. The future projections can also be shared.

Deal

This will contain the amount required and the equity dilution which the founders are looking for in lieu of the investment.

Thus, you can see that pitch decks are an important part of communicating facts about a startup to the investors. A good pitch deck is an important necessity in getting funding from professional investors. Both angel investors and venture capitalists require a pitch deck. The only difference between pitch decks for angel investors and VCs is that during the early stage the product may not be ready, and financials may not be there. Some of the other details like the market size may also be not as clear as in later stages. Thus, pitch deck for early-stage investors may be less detailed and more concise.

I would also recommend the startup entrepreneurs to read some books and see some videos on presentation design. I have been a judge in many startup pitching competitions and my experience is that most people try to cram too many details in a slide. Once I was a judge in IIM Lucknow pitching competition and to my surprise, most teams created slides that looked like word documents. They were very information heavy. Ideally, visual thinking should be used, and slides should have relevant visuals along with relevant points.

I would recommend books like **Presentation Zen**, **The Back of the Napkin** and books and videos by *Nancy Duarte* to learn more about creating good presentations. The heart of human beings can only be reached using stories. Thus, many of the famous authors who teach about presentations tell about presenting using storytelling. I have personally worked with *Vijay Shekhar Sharma* of Paytm. He is a great storyteller and has great convincing power. That ability is really a big reason for Paytm's growth.

Thus, if you want funding a great pitch deck is a must. You will not be able to create a great pitch deck in one shot. It is an iterative process. Over time you will be able to iterate to a great pitch deck. When combined with visual thinking and great storytelling your probability of getting investment will be greatly increased.

What is a 'term sheet'

When an investor like a professional angel investor or venture capitalist invests in a startup, they follow a process. The process generally involves pitching followed by follow-up meetings. If the investor is convinced that this startup is good for investing, then the investor signs a term sheet with the startup founders.

Figure 4.10: *Term Sheet*

The term sheet may be a binding or non-binding agreement that lists the terms and conditions for making the investment. After signing the term sheet, the investor does due diligence on the startup. Once due diligence is complete the investor and the startup execute final binding legal documents.

The term sheet generally signifies that the investor is willing to invest at a particular valuation. The complexity of the term sheet depends on the size of the funding round and the type of investor. Angels usually have simpler term sheets than VCs. Many investors have standard term sheets which they keep as a base while negotiating.

The term sheet is also a legal document and thus I will recommend you take the advice of a qualified **lawyer** or a **Chartered Accountant (CA)** who has expertise in them before signing them. General lawyers and CA do not have that expertise. Only selected professionals who specialize in startup matters have this expertise.

I am listing some of the terms and conditions which are generally covered under the **Term Sheet**. This is not legal advice, but my intention is to give you some head start in understanding term sheets before you negotiate with the investor and engage the professionals. Also, a big reason I am sharing these terms with you is that without knowing these terms, funding looks very glamorous. Media covers funding news in a way that it feels that funding is not an obligation to investors but is like winning a prize.

The following are the terms generally covered in a term sheet:

Legal details

This entails:

- Name and identification details of investors, startup, and its founders
- Date of the term sheet
- Legal jurisdiction applicable in case of dispute

Entry terms

This entails:

- **Valuation**: Pre-money valuation (valuation of startup before taking money from investor) accepted by the investor
- **Investment and milestones**: The amount to be invested in the startup by investors. The amount may be invested at one go or

it may be as per pre-specified milestones. Generally, the first tranche is given on execution of final binding documents and completion of conditions precedent.

- **Shareholding**: Shareholding pattern of the company pre-investment and after each milestone. This is also called the **capital table (cap table)** of the company.
- **Type of securities and price per unit**: Even though equity is given to investors, due to legal and practical reasons direct share allotment is not done. Generally, in India investors prefer either **Compulsory Convertible Debentures (CCD)** or **Compulsory Convertible Preference Shares (CCPS)**. Y Combinator (famous US startup accelerator) prefers using **Simple Agreement For Future Equity (SAFE)**. The price per unit is also mentioned in the term sheet.
- **Use of funds**: It is mentioned that the investment proceeds will be used to achieve the pre-decided business plan and the milestones decided between investors and the founders.
- **Exclusivity**: This clause says that the founders or the startup cannot raise capital from any other investor for the 'period of exclusivity' after signing the term sheet. The period of exclusivity is generally up to 90 days and may vary according to the investor. I know of investors who have this as 60 days also.
- **Conditions precedent**: These are generally conditions that need to be fulfilled before any money will be transferred to the startup by the investor. They mostly relate to the completion of due diligence and legal processes. It may also involve the transfer of intellectual property (IP) to the startup from the name of founders.
- **Conditions subsequent**: These are conditions that need to be fulfilled as soon as money is received by the startup. Some examples of such conditions are:
    - Appointment of auditors agreed by investors
    - Issue of securities
    - Legal process-related
    - Formulation of ESOP scheme

Exit terms

Liquidation Preferences: The liquidation preference clause tells who will get the money first and in what quantum in case of a liquidation event for the startup. A liquidation event is basically the closure, sale, or merger of a startup.

1x liquidation preference means the investor gets the original investment amount back first before anything is given to the founders or other shareholders. Generally, in the early stages 1x liquidation preference clause is there. In the late stages of financing, it may be 1.5x or even 2x. It can be any number decided by the company and the investors.

Liquidation preference is of 2 types:

- o **Non-participating**: The investor has the preference to choose between taking the liquidation preference and getting money before it is distributed between shareholders in the ratio of their holding or take the money according to the normal shareholding pattern but not both.
- o **Participating**: Here the investor has the best of both. The investor takes liquidation preference and gets money invested according to the liquidation preference ratio before it is distributed to shareholders in the shareholding ratio. The investor also takes money again when it is distributed according to his or her holding in the shareholding ratio. This is very rare in term sheets.

- **Transfer rights**: The investors can sell their shares at any time. The founders will not be allowed to sell their shares during the lock-in period. Moreover, after lock-in finishes, the founders can only sell their shares after the permission of the majority of investors. However, this sale of shares will be bound by the **tag-along rights** of investors and the **Right Of First Refusal (ROFR).**
- **Exit rights and exit strategy**: The investors invest to multiply their capital. The investors usually only get money back on the sale of their shares to 3rd parties. Thus, investors put a time period in the term sheet whereby they put an obligation on the founders to find a buyer for their shares, or do an Initial Public Offering (IPO), or buy back their shares.

In case the founders are not able to do any of these then the investor would have the right to sell the shares to any buyer they like and have the right to drag along the founders and other shareholders to sell their shares.

Also in the event, even this is not possible or there is some breach of trust by the founders the investor would have the right to take money after getting a high interest or in worst case scenario the founders and other promoters will have to give all their shares to investors at face value meaning that practically they will be getting pennies for their entire shareholding.

This is a major clause and founders should take funding keeping in mind that in the worst-case scenario they will get practically nothing in the company.

Management terms

This entails:

- **Founder rights**: Generally, founders need to sign a lock-in clause. The founders will not be able to sell shares to anyone without investor permission till a specified time, which is generally 4 years.

  Sometimes the shares are also vested to founders as per a mechanism listed in the term sheet. On day 1 they may start with 0 shares. A popular method is to give 25% shares after first 12 months and 1/48th shares every month thereafter for the next 36 months.

- **ESOP pool**: Investors understand that the core team of the company and future employees of the company will be motivated and retained by ESOPs. Thus, most term sheets will have a clause on ESOP pool creation. This generally ranges from 7.5% to 10% on equity share capital post-funding. The ESOP pool is from the equity of the founders and investors specifically mention that their shareholding will not be diluted for the ESOP pool.

- **Board**: Generally, investors want the right to nominate at least 1 board member. Moreover, many times investors want to appoint 1 board observer also. These rights are thus written in a term sheet.

- **Voting rights**: The investor generally will write that the investor will have voting rights on a fully diluted basis. Also, some investors will also write that some specific things will need mandatory consent of the investor director in the board.

Investor rights

The investors generally want the following rights:

- **Right of first refusal**: Whenever the founders sell their shares to someone, they will have to give the option to the investor to buy the shares first. This clause may be applicable to other non-investor shareholders also.
- **Tag-along right**: After the completion of lock-in, if the founders sell equity shares to someone else then the investor can force them to sell investor's shares also at the same price.
- **Drag along right**: If the founders cannot provide exit to the investor after a set number of years, the investor can sell the shares to any buyer and drag along the founders to sell to that buyer at that rate.
- **Auditors**: Investors generally want to have a say in appointing an auditor. Some term sheets specifically mention auditor appointment rights.
- **Rights in future rounds**: Generally anti-dilution rights are mentioned in the term sheet.
- **Restricted items**: The terms may list items which will only be allowed subject to consent of the investor nominated director. The founders and CEO are not allowed to decide on these matters on their own.

Should I take funding

Most people like money. Media attaches a lot of glamour to getting funding. Thus, most entrepreneurs attach a lot of importance to getting funding. Funding is useful to grow the business, but funding has lots of attached conditions.

Startup funding is not like a jackpot. It has a lot of attached responsibilities. The investor gives funding because he or she wants to grow the money at least 10-20 times. This puts enormous pressure on entrepreneurs to deliver growth.

Figure 4.11: *Should I take funding?*

Moreover, funding is a complex process, and the entrepreneur needs to devote a lot of time out of business towards getting funding. This wastes a lot of time of the entrepreneurs as majority investors decline funding the startup. Many successful startups got funding after meeting tens of investors.

Investors also put in lots of terms and conditions upon the startup and the entrepreneurs when they fund the startup. This also means that investors generally will be the first ones to get the money on sale of a startup to a big organization. In many cases entrepreneurs do not get anything if the startup is not super successful.

Thus, entrepreneurs should not get attached to the glamour attached with funding and think about funding from a detached point of view. Entrepreneurs should get funding from angel investors only after problem solution fit so that at least the direction of the startup is clear. Many times, entrepreneurs feel frustrated when investors impose their thoughts about markets and products on them.

If the startup has got product market fit and needs money to grow, then getting funding from venture capitalists is the way to go. There is no doubt that external investors can help startups to grow fast through their contacts, mentoring and money.

Thus, take money only when you feel comfortable working with the investor, and you feel that the investor will add value to your startup besides just providing money. Mentoring and networking are some of the biggest benefits of getting funded. Furthermore, media coverage after funding is also extremely useful and will give your business the required exposure.

Thus, taking funding has its own benefits but entrepreneurs need to be cautious while taking funding.

What if I fail

Many entrepreneurs do not start a startup because they are afraid of failing. In my own experience even if you fail 100%, there are lots of ways to grow your career as a startup founder.

Figure 4.12: *What if I fail?*

The worst-case scenario is a super-duper flop startup which burns your hard-earned savings. Another worst-case scenario is co-founders or investors conspiring against you and kicking you out of your own startup. Even in that case the experience of running a startup will give you growth in your career. Lots of successful entrepreneurs like *Vijay Shekhar Sharma* of Paytm give preference to failed entrepreneurs while recruiting for senior positions. I know someone who was kicked out of his startup by his co-founder and investor wrongfully but got a senior job in Paytm due to that experience.

There are cases where the startup is not successful, and investors want to sell it to a bigger company. In that case even though the entrepreneur is not very happy selling out, they generally earn handsomely unless there is a slump sale or super bear market is going on.

Running a startup is one of the best learning experiences in the world. It makes you tough and mentally agile. It will also teach you 10 times more than the best degrees, you can get.

Many of the senior most people in the technology industry were founders of startups which failed. Thus, an entrepreneur should analyze the pros and cons of starting a startup but should not be very anxious or scared of failing. Moreover, following the startup best practices will increase your odds of success.

Conclusion

We learned that startup founders initially need to bootstrap the startup. After that once problem solution fit is found they can approach the professional angel investors. These days even startup incubators and government provide some funding to startups. Multiple investors need to be reached for getting a successful investment. After achieving product market fit a startup can reach out to venture capitalists for funding.

A startup needs to prepare a good elevator pitch and a pitch deck. Once the investors are interested in funding a startup, they sign a term sheet with the startup. After that they do a detailed due diligence and finally sign detailed legal documents before providing funding to the startup.

CHAPTER 5

Conclusion: When Should I Start a Startup

Startups can be opened at any age. While *Bill Gates* and *Mark Zuckerberg* started at a very young age, *Henry Ford* started Ford Motor at a relatively mature age. There is no right or wrong age for beginning a startup.

***Figure 5.1:** When Should I Start A Startup?*

Generally, I think that it is the easiest way to start a startup in college, especially in India. In college, parents do not push an entrepreneur to support the family. In fact, parents are happy to support the entrepreneur while he or she is still in college. These days many colleges have e-cells (entrepreneurship cells) and incubators to support student startups. At times professors and friends are also supportive during college days. The best thing about starting a startup in college is that if the startup does not work in the first few months, you can always find a regular job after college.

However, if after college, you start a startup, it becomes a little more difficult. The entrepreneur has to handle peer pressure and family responsibilities. I would advise that entrepreneurs who have passed college should do 1-2 jobs after college before starting a startup. Jobs will help you save some money for the initial capital in your startup and give you some real-world experience.

Another good age for starting a startup is around 40. You are more experienced at that time and have good connections. Moreover, you get time to save money for bootstrapping. Thus 40 is a good age for starting a startup. I started my most recent startup when I was 40 years old.

I had an uncle who was very entrepreneurial and wanted to start a startup in his 70s. Thus, being an entrepreneur is more about passion and your mindset rather than about your physical age.

You should open a startup when you feel you have found a big problem which you can solve. You have some money to bootstrap your startup for at least 1 year and you feel that you cannot live without starting your startup. Open a startup when your passion for starting a startup is running high.

Index

A

B

C